Medford

Medford, Oregon - Spring 1996
Photo by Bert Webber

Bear Creek, a major tributary of the Rogue River, flows from south to north through Medford on its way to join the river. Although everyone talks about Medford being in the "Rogue River Valley," the city is actually in Bear Creek Valley. (LOWER) Medford Irrigation District dam near Jackson Street bridge. This dam will be removed over the next few years to improve creek flow through center of the city.

The Lure of
Medford

—An Oregon Documentary—
Bert and Margie Webber

WEBB RESEARCH GROUP PUBLISHERS
Books About the Oregon Country

Published by
WEBB RESEARCH GROUP PUBLISHERS
Books About the Oregon Country
P. O. Box 314 Medford OR 97501

Cover photographs
Front: Camera faces east at
Central Avenue and W. Main Street
Back: Schoenstein Pipe Organ in
First Presbyterian Church

Photographs are by the authors or are from
the authors' collection unless otherwise credited

Cataloging-in-Publication Data:

Webber, Bert
    The lure of Medford : documentary / Bert and Margie Webber
    p.   cm.
    Includes bibliographical references and index.
    ISBN 0-936738-47-2
    1. Medford (Or.)–History. I. Webber, Margie. II. Title.
F884. W   1996
979.5'27
                                 L.C. #
                                 forthcoming

Contents

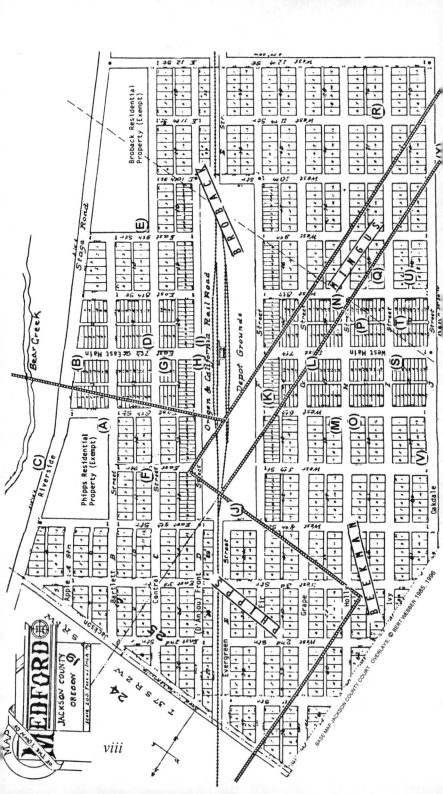

viii

Introduction

Medford (42° 20' N Latitude - 122° 52' W Longitude) grew from a small town with unpaved streets to become, in a little over a century, the trade and medical center of southern Oregon and northern California.

It all started with the Oregon and California Railroad. The railroad wanted to establish its Rogue Valley base in an already established community, but when arrangements with a nearby community could worked out, the engineers decided to build their own town. That town became Medford.

The town didn't start as the charming place it has grown to be. The site is in the Agate Desert which is generally described as a large acreage of rocky soil, dry-land weeds, rabbits, grass-hoppers and rattlesnakes. But Medford thrived and, over time, has covered a lot of the desert with all sorts of buildings, as-phalt, and many lush green yards.

IDENTIFICATIONS FOR MAP ON OPPOSITE PAGE

Original plat of Medford, Oregon showing the four property holders' original land overlaid on city blocks and streets. Each man held considerably more land that extended beyond the limits of the city. Original streets east-to-west were letters "A" "B" "C" etc. renamed later as shown. 7th Street became Main Street and was originally blocked by the railroad station. Some of today's prominent sites shown in bold face letters

A Greyhound Depot	M Holly Theater Bldg.
B Hubbard's Hardware	N Presbyterian Church
C Red Lion Motel	O Federal Bldg.
D Mini-park	P Alba Park
E Used car lot	Q Post Office
F Elk's Lodge	R Catholic School
G U.S. National Bank	S Medford Hotel
H 1st Interstate Bank	T Public Library
I Key Bank	U City Hall
J Goodwill Industries	V Episcopal Church
H *Mail Tribune*	W County Court House
L Pacific Light & Power Co.	X Catholic Church

Base Map - Jackson County Court. Overlays Copyright Bert Webber Feb. 1985 / July 1996

The writers have wanted to do a trilogy of books about Southern Oregon. For the town to the west, the phrase

Jacksonville Oregon; Antique Town in a Modern Age
–Documentary –

became that book's title. The title for the book about the unique town to the south became

Ashland – An Oregon Oasis – An Oregon Documentary.

How to describe Medford was the question? The title:

The Lure of Medford – Documentary

kept coming to the top in the suggestion box so we have used it.

But what could this "lure" be? Some say it's the shopping centers and the excellent medical installations but these factors are of fairly recent vintage. What was the "lure" long before these facilities came into being? After a lot of brainstorming, it was finally concluded that the "lure" could only be the weather.

The good weather permits a substantial agricultural establishment, primarily great pears. Outdoor recreation throughout the immediate region has grown beyond earlier expectations and covers a range of activities from golf, swimming, hiking, mountain climbing, fishing, hunting, and in the winter – skiing.

To cite a lot of statistics from the National Weather Service can be boring reading and sounds like a promotion from a Chamber of Commerce. We just say that Medford has amazingly bright and warm springs, summers and autumns, and mild winters. There are rainy spells in spring and fall. Some summer days often get above 100 degrees but the humidity is low. High temperature does not seem to slow down most of the people as offices, stores, many homes, and most cars, are air conditioned.

Winters seldom see snow on the valley floor, but when it comes, the snow doesn't usually last very long. (An occasional winter snow storm can be a doozie.) In the dead of winter, many people in Medford are unable to see very far as there may be a heavy fog that settles in the Rogue River Valley. We have some unique information about fog, and measures to be rid of it, in the airport chapters.

Oregon has a reputation of being a rainy state but there is a minimum of rain in Medford, only 19 inches a year. When one hears about the "constant rain in western Oregon" and the joke about Oregonians who grow "webs" between their toes due to all that rain, one must exclude Medford from these labels as Medford is part of Oregon's "banana belt." This is because the weather phenomena in the Rogue Valley is more often linked to that of the hot Sacramento Valley of California instead of that of western Oregon.

The Rogue Valley, which averages about 1,300 elevation feet above sea level, is sheltered from "western" Oregon weather by a ring of mountains. On the west the mountains are about 2,500 feet elevation while on the north, the ring of peaks rise to 3,834 feet for Sexton Mountain. Mount McLoughlin to the east, towers at 9,495 feet and looks like a giant ice cream cone with its snow cap all spring. Brown Mountain, south of McLoughlin, is 7,311 feet elevation. To the south are the Siskiyou Mountains topped off by Mt. Ashland at 7,533 feet high, where there is an extensive winter ski area. With all this protection, Medford's "lure" is the favorable weather and the activities that suitable weather affords.

During winter snow storms in the mountains, there can be challenges at times for access in and out of Medford. On the north, the freeway goes through Sexton Mountain Pass at 1,970 feet elevation. That's just high enough to sometimes require "traction devices" for about ten miles of the 278 miles to Portland. To get to Klamath Falls, 76 miles east, one drives over the pass on highway 140, between Mt. McLoughlin and Brown Mountain at 5,510 feet. In winter, this road is often icy and is sometimes closed.

The challenge, especially for the plethora of long, heavy trucks on Interstate-5 coming to and from Medford on the south, is the steep pass at 4,310 feet. The Oregon/California border is just 29 miles south of Medford and in bad winters, the freeway can be closed for several days at a time due to heavy snow, ice, or thick fog. On some days, chains might be required. But the locals know about the weather's doings as the forecasts are clearly shown on the three major networks' television stations in

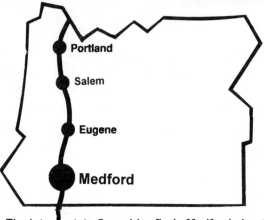

The Interstate-5 corridor finds Medford about mid-way between Portland and Sacramento.

Medford several times a day.

The weather. Once cannot do anything about it but hate or love it. We've not met anyone in Medford who truly hates it.

Our book deals with some of the "lures" that have brought people to Medford in the past as well as to the present time. These can be determined at a glance by looking at the Table of Contents. We have tried to bring some of Medford's highlights but there too many to list them all.

Just about everybody in Medford knows about the airport for that is the major "people-mover" in and out of the valley, other than in private automobiles. Trains with passenger service quit in 1955. About that time, to drive a car to Portland took between 10 and 12 hours due to the narrow, twisting, road called highway 99. The train took nearly the same time. Highways and the train track seemed to pass through the center of nearly every hamlet, village, town and city along the way. Then came the completion of the freeway – Interstate-5 – in the mid-1960's.

The Oregon State Police advertised if one made the distance between Medford and Portland in less than 4 hours and 5 minutes, one was "speeding." The speed limit then was 70 mph. Although the limit presently is 65, the increased traffic is called "terrific" thus five to six hours to Portland is common. The bus takes about the same time. By commercial airline, the flight is about one hour.

There are a lot of things people take for granted about airports. We have delved into the history of the Medford airport

Actress Ginger Rogers first appeared on the Craterian Theater stage in 1926 with her group "Ginger Rogers and The Redheads." She was 15. Her final appearance on the Craterian stage was at a fund-raiser in November 1993 when she lent her name and support to the project of renovating the structure into a performing arts center. She called Medford her home. She died April 25, 1995.

and believe we have come up with some items that the public, even the old timers, may have missed or maybe forgotten about it and of course, the newcomers will learn about them here for the first time. A couple of examples: Medford was the first city in Oregon to have air mail service. Another: Charles A. Lindbergh, the pilot who was the first to fly alone across the Atlantic Ocean, flew over Medford in his ocean-hopping Ryan airplane one day and did little more than look down. But he was on the ground at the Medford airport twice, later. We'll tell you about the "Lone Eagle" – Lindbergh – and his stops in Medford.

On the cultural side, we present sketches of the musical effort in Medford. Its symphony, its chorale, its concert band and the Community Concerts – all always popular.

Further about music. In looking over many books about various towns, we have never found one that has anything to say about pipe organs. We include pipe organs here for in the 1920's, a never-to-be-forgotten pipe organ salesman hit the town. We'll explain.

Movie Actress Ginger Rogers claimed Medford as her home, which was actually a working ranch, along the beautiful Rogue River, a little north of town. "Miss Ginger" fell right in with the local folks and was seen carrying her own shopping basket in the stores. She made many "official" public appearances, particularly during World War-II, when she promoted war bond sales at street rallies. When she died recently, many of

Medford's Craterian Theater, is being totally renovated and has been renamed the Craterian Ginger Rogers Thearer. The work will take several years to complete.

the people were saddened. Shortly thereafter, the old Craterian Theater, which is in process of major renovation to become a performing arts center, was renamed for Miss Ginger. It will be the Craterian Ginger Rogers Theater.

Medford's newspaper, the *Mail Tribune* is, in people terms, a senior citizen. This year marks the 90th birthday for the *Mail Tribune* which has the unique distinction of having been awarded a Pulitzer Prize. The newspaper has expanded its facilities several times in an effort to keep up with community growth.

There is radio and television. KMED (AM radio) started broadcasting in 1922 and is Oregon's first commercial station. It is still going strong. There are additional AM and FM stations.

KOBI-TV Channel 5, went on the air as KBES-TV in August 1958 and it was the first VHF television station in Oregon. From its facilities in Medford, Channel 5 translators reach out to distant population centers and rural areas over a wide arc of southern Oregon and northern California.

KSYS-TV, the public television station, went on the air January 1, 1977. It is a favorite of many, is community supported.

"One-log load" with the woods crew pose for visiting photographer. It is rare now to see such a sight.

Medford and the southern Oregon counties do not receive any signals from Portland broadcasters (not even by cable at this writing), and seldom any AM stations even at night. Medford may be isolated by many miles and hours of driving from the population centers of the Willamette Valley, but it has radio and television outlets for all three national networks, ABC, CBS, NBC and there is a television cable service.

For years, the major industries in the Medford area have been the timber business and the fruit orchards. Currently, tourism has become a major factor. As the decades of history of these businesses have been well covered elsewhere, we will not dwell on them here. With a switch to liberal environmentalism, to the detriment of employment of thousands in the timber cutting and wood processing business, that business has suffered to the point where many once major mills have closed and a number of the huge lumber mills have been dismantled.*

The tourist industry is very good as evidenced by a large number of travel agencies in the telephone book. Due to the strategic location of the airport, Medford is the center of the Rogue River Valley for travelers, be they in the valley as vacationers or on business.

With the opening of the freeway, thousands of people, largely from the "sunny south," have used Interstate-5 and "found" Medford although the city was never "lost."

* Refer to *This is Logging and Sawmilling* in bibliography

15

Medford's post office has had a challenge in keeping up with the area's expansion. This influx of people has brought an increase to the number of letter carriers for the city and on the rural routes. The post office is now a Sectional Center servicing a vast number of ZIP codes. The local zones presently include:

97501   Medford (city and rural west side)
97502   Central Point Branch (north of town)
97503   White City Branch (northeast of town)
97504   Medford (city and rural east side)

People from far distances entered southern Oregon first by the Applegate Trail, also called the "southern route" (1846), by stage coach (1850's - early 1880's), then by trains (1887), by highway 99 (1920's - 30's), and by the freeway (1960's). Many stopped here. Many stayed.

Population in Medford city limits shows this growth:			
1884 (established)		1950	17,305
1890	967	1960	24,425
1900	1,791	1970	28,973
1910*	8,840	1980	39,603
1920*	5,756	1990	46,951
1930	11,007	1995	55,090
1940	11,281	1996	57,000 est.

*The populations for 1910 and 1920 would appear to be reversed, however, research back to the original documents have the numbers as shown here. (Ed.) —Population Abstract of the United States

More people settled in Medford in the five years between 1990 and 1995 than settled here during the entire the decade of the 1980's. And they are still coming.

It is good to publish the names and thank the principals who have assisted with the research for this book.

The primary investigator for the Charles A. Lindbergh visits to Medford was Richard E. Webber, Stratford, N.J. Rick has been a Lindbergh enthusiast and radio-control model airplane pilot from his earliest years. Our thanks to eldest son, Rick.

We appreciate the interest of career newspaper writers and editors Peggy Ann Hutchinson and Cleve Twitchell of the *Mail Tribune*. Ms. Hutchinson was willing to answer many questions and provided material from her files. Twitchell, who has offered a friendly ear to us over a long period, provides that special encouragement just at the right time. We thank these fellow journalists and hold them in high esteem.

. Anne Billeter, Ph.D., head of Adult Services at the Medford Branch of the Jackson County Library Services, and her staff of reference librarians, have assisted in locating and verifying many details that have found their way into this book. We appreciate their assistance which has been friendly as well as professional.

We are indebted to the folks at the Reuter Pipe Organ Company, Lawrence, Kansas, who willingly assisted with our chapter on pipe organs. We are thankful to Lauren T. Webber, Lynn, Massachusetts, our youngest son, who for a time was with the Rogers Organ Company of New England. His insight and help with the general subject of pipe organs was eye-opening to us and we acknowledge his help.

The research into the architecture of the late Frank C. Clark was greatly assisted by the long-standing endeavors of Rosalyn R. Rhinehart. Her work has been a labor of love and over the years she has been able to locate nearly every site in Medford where stands, or stood, a Frank Clark designed building. On this same subject, we appreciate the assistance of Carol Harbison Samuelson at the Library of the Southern Oregon Historical Society who helped identify sites and photographs. What we believe to be the most comprehensive list of locations ever compiled for popular use, is in the Appendix of this book.

There were many more individuals and organizations who provided assistance and answers to many of our questions. We acknowledge their help collectively.

The authors welcome letters of constructive comments which may be sent in care of the publisher, but regret the inability to make individual replies. The address is listed on page *vi*.

Bert and Margie Webber
Spring 1996

Looking northeasterly from Main and Fir Streets in the early days. Date of picture unknown. The two men (arrow) are walking the track which is nearly covered with mud from the unpaved street. During this period there were no "pooper-scoopers" that followed horses.

1

Who Started Medford?

Medford, the metropolis of Southern Oregon, was not the first settlement in the area by a long shot. When those two fellows discovered gold in what became Jacksonville, in 1851, there were no settlements in the Rogue River Valley other than Indian villages.

Medford was founded because of railroad interests and then, only because the village of Central Point, four miles north of Medford, would not make a deal with the railroad people. The Oregon and California Railroad topographical engineers sought to build a line from Portland into California by way of the Rogue River Valley. Central Point, being about in the center of the valley, seemed a likely place to build a station and a switch yard. The only other consideration was Ashland, but that location was for a roundhouse and repair facilities. Trains about to climb the Siskiyou Mountains, and those descending, needed a service point at the base of the mountain – Ashland would handle that. But Ashland was considered too far from the chugging through the mountains north of Medford for a simple switchyard. Central Point, founded in 1852 by Isaac Constant, where stage roads crossed in the center of the valley – hence the name – was the engineer's choice.

The story, according to tradition, was that the engineers called for a meeting with the few people of the Central Point vicinity. The O&C men wanted some "donations" to assure that the track would be laid through Central Point and in exchange, the railroad would install the switchyard there. All trains would stop thus the village would prosper because of trade generated by the railroad. This was the logic used in hundreds of similar deals along nearly every railroad line during the westward expansion.

Main Street looking east from about Fir Street. Passenger train in depot was headed south. Date of picture is unknown but it had to be after 1911 because the Baldwin locomotive number, readable with a jeweler's glass, No. 2347, was built that year.

Agate Desert in summer where star thistles thrive.

The men of the village would not bend to the railroader's plans so the O&C representatives left the meeting, decided to built their own town and allow Central Point to die on the vine. When the track was eventually laid, it missed Central Point by about one mile to the west. (Not to be outsmarted, the Central Pointers moved their town to the railroad!)

Four miles south of Central Point was a wild and wide spot in the Agate Desert. It was heavily inhabited with rabbits, rattle-snakes, crickets and desert-like flora. The only thing going for the site was Bear Creek which flowed through the center of the valley from the base of the Siskiyou Mountains to the Rogue River. The railroad men would build their own town from scratch at this site.

In the meantime, the village of Jacksonville prospered be-cause of the gold rush. It became the largest settlement in Jack-son County and the county seat. It was five miles west of the eventual Medford site and six miles, on an angle, from Central Point. When word seeped into the ears of the Jacksonvillians that "the railroad is coming," the natural conclusion was to prepare for the arrival of the track in Jacksonville. After all, it *was* the seat of the county and it was a thriving town. But when track-laying time arrived, the rails missed Jacksonville. Let's see why?

In 1855, the U.S. Army Corps of Topographical Engineers was engaged in several surveys to recommend locations for railroads. The survey of interest was the route from Benecia, California, east of San Francisco on the Sacramento River, to Portland and return. It was a massive effort. The report of this survey appears in *Senate Executive Document No., 78*, 33rd Congress 2d Session, 1857. The official title of the part of the survey that concerns the Rogue River Valley in Oregon carries the title:

> *Report of Lieut. Henry Abbot, Corps of Topographical Engineers Upon Explorations For A Railroad Route, from the Sacramento Valley to the Columbia River Made By Lieut. R. S. Williamson, Corps of Topographical Engineers, Assisted by Lieut. Henry L. Abbot, Corps of Topographical Engineers — 1855.*

Lt. Williamson's orders stated he was to include geological information, accurate observation of the character of the country, nature of difficulties encountered and quality and extent of building materials to be found. Further, be was to observe the botany and natural history and such other objects as tend to illustrate the conditions. He was authorized to be issued scientific instruments from the warehouse of the Topographical Engineers, but if not available, to buy on the market such scientific instruments as required.

You are authorized to hire a geologist, a civil engineer, a computer [mathematician-astronomer] a draughtsman and a physician who will at the same time perform as a naturalist or geologist.

Lt. Williamson led the expedition on the northward trek which entered Oregon in the vicinity of Klamath Falls.

The route was northerly to check out the Deschutes Valley as a potential railroad route. At a point in the Bend area, Lt. Williamson detached himself and went west into the Willamette Valley thence to Portland. Lt. Abbot, who was officially second in command of the exploring detachment, became the valiant

Henry Larcom Abbot U.S. Army Corps of Topographical Engineers.
—West Point Archives

leader of the scientists and escort troops (needed because of encounters with Indians). He continued north for a way then cut northwest for Portland. It had been presumed that a railroad route crossing the state in Central Oregon was impractical with the technology of the time. The survey validated that belief.

Lt. Williamson, being ordered to San Francisco by ship, left the remainder of the expedition of railroad survey, from Portland south, to Lt. Abbot. In short order, Lt. Abbot turned his men toward California and was confronted with an order that took his escort of armed troops from his expedition. His concern was because of deadly skirmishes with Indians in Southern Oregon that had become out-of-hand.

The trip up the Willamette Valley was of no special note. From the location of Canyonville, be followed the Applegate Trail of 1846 through the beautiful Canyon Creek drainage to the divide, then descended into the Rogue River Valley near Grants Pass.

As mentioned, the Rogue Indian Wars were in progress. From a point at Fort Lane, on the Rogue River, the surveyors set their mark for the Siskiyou Mountains. The valley was mostly

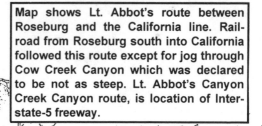

Map shows Lt. Abbot's route between Roseburg and the California line. Railroad from Roseburg south into California followed this route except for jog through Cow Creek Canyon which was declared to be not as steep. Lt. Abbot's Canyon Creek Canyon route, is location of Interstate-5 freeway.

ROSEBURG

Myrtle Creek

South Umpqua River

Cow Creek Canyon

CANYONVILLE

UMPQUA MOUNTAINS

Cow Cr.

SIX-BIT HOUSE
(RENAMED WOLF CREEK)

ROGUE RIVER

RIVER

Hamil Rancho

timbered Ridges

Table Rock

FORT LANE

JACKSONVILLE

Applegate Creek

UNEXPLORED

SISKIYOU MOUNTAINS Pilot Rock

open ground and slightly upslope along Bear Creek therefore the trip through the Indian-risk area was made "with facility" – fast – recalling that his soldiers had been withdrawn, which left the expedition without protection.

The actual building of the railroad did not occur for some time. When the track was laid as far as Eugene, debates occurred where a faction wanted the line to cross on Lt. Williamson's route to Central Oregon and go to California, retracing the northward trek of the topographical engineers. Others wanted the route to California to be via the Rogue River Valley following Lt. Abbot's southbound survey. It took the effort of U. S. Senator George H. Williams (R-Oregon 1865-1871) to push for and decide the route. It would be through the Rogue Valley. We shall investigate more about this shortly.

This was the time when the Jacksonville folks made their plans to receive the railroad. Apparently, no one in Jacksonville had ever heard of the 1855 survey and that J-ville had been left out. Some of the J-folks wanted to bribe the railroad site-planning engineers. The word was passed around that the town needed to donate a station and yard site and hand over $25,000 in cash. The story went that with this "blackmail," the track would be routed through Jacksonville.

1. Was it a sound idea?
2. Did anyone have the money?
3. Would The Beekman Bank in Jacksonville loan the money?

The answer to the three questions was:

1. No!
2. No!
3. No!

When it comes to building a railroad, the matter of who owns the land it will run on must be considered. Some Jacksonville property owners had planned on making a killing when they sold rights-of-way for the track. At least one did, but as shall see, it was not in Jacksonville.

If the decision where to route the track was totally up to the field engineers of the railroad, a proposition by some men who

25

Southern Pacific Company map of January 1927 demonstrates the two routes established by the Corps of Engineers in 1855. The debate, once rails had been laid to Eugene, was to choose Lt. Williamson's route over the Cascade Mountains into the high-desert by way of Klamath Falls to California or, Lt. Abbot's route through the Unpqua and Rogue River Valleys to the Siskiyou Mountains into California. The Siskiyou route was chosen. Later resurveys showed that Lt. Williamson's route was faster and easier on locomotives. SP opened its Natron Route by way of Klamath Falls in 1926. Today's AMTRAK trains use the Natron route. The Siskiyou route was sold by SP in 1995 to Rail-Tex which operates its Central Oregon and Pacific trains, presently freight only, over the Siskiyou Mountains.

Questions ?

Was there any notice by the public, or of official Jacksonville, of the fairly large size railroad expedition working in the vicinity, and did anyone question why the topographical engineers did not stop in the county seat at least for a cup of tea?

The authors chose what they believe to be two excellent documents of the time to look at that question.

1). The diary of Welborn Beeson *
2). Jacksonville's newspaper, the *Table Rock Sentinel*.

1). Welborn Beeson was a young farmer who lived with his father (John Beeson) and his mother, on the family farm. He had kept a diary since his 16th birthday and would do so until his dying day. His diary is considered unique by researchers because his entries cover several decades. On the days Lt. Abbot's command was striding parallel to Bear Creek, Beeson wrote:

Monday. Mr. Nailor is very sick. Sam Robinson and I sat up with him all night. Father and I went to Jacksonville. I got one pr of pants, 1 pr boots, 1 shirt. Been a cool day.

Had there been any reports of the surveyors passing near the Beeson place, which was not very far distant from Bear Creek along which the expedition followed, it would seem that someone would have mentioned it to Welborn and he would have included it in his diary. One the next day. He entered:

Tuesday. It rained. Went hunting. Nailor is some better.

2). A search was made on the microfilm of the *Table Rock Sentinel* to see of Editor William G. T'Vault mentioned the survey party or its mission. We noted first, that when the party traveled up the valley, the newspaper was not yet born. Its first issue was November 14, just over one week after the railroad survey expedition passed five miles to the east. With such an unusual event as a railroad survey through the valley, and the potential business to be generated in a town by a railroad, this would have been front page news. But T'Vault's paper made no mention of topographical engineers being in the area.

As we have seen, the engineers went up the Bear Creek Valley heading for the safety of Siskiyou Mountains in such haste to get away from any encounter with the Indians, the company did not even stop on the way for lunch.

---

* Refer to bibliography for the Beeson diary.

owned some land near Bear Creek might have persuaded them. One of these men was Cornelius C. Beekman, the banker of Jacksonville. The others were Conrad Mingus, Ira J. Phipps and C. W. Broback.

These gents pooled their interests and platted a townsite in the Agate Desert, five miles east of Jacksonville. There would be a grand payoff to guarantee that the new railroad would be just where these men wanted it. They donated 1,240 acres as a personal gift to the field engineer in charge of the O.& C. survey. Then they donated an extra twenty acres to the railroad for a station and switch yard, plus every other block within the townsite. In all, the railroad received 41 city blocks. Many of the people thought they saw a connection. Some chose to believe that Beekman wouldn't loan money to bring the track to Jacksonville because if he did, he wouldn't be able to make his deal at trackside to the railroad. With a deal as good as this, why should a railroad detour by way of Jacksonville?

When the final papers were drawn on December 22, 1883, 19.86 acres were donated to the railroad. Just one day earlier, an edition of the Ashland *Tidings* recorded there were piles of lumber in various places in the new townsite and several buildings had already gone up.

But there were other considerations for leaving out Jacksonville. Railroads like to build track in straight lines for straight track costs less to build and to maintain. And, there were productive farms along the straight right-of-way. The O. & C,. was running short of money and while it would be polite to jog the rails in that direction, Jacksonville had no economic base from which to generate freight.

In addition, the entire line from the Rogue River was upgrade all the way to the California line. Why huff and puff by way of Jacksonville over a route that would have to navigate around some hills on the west side of the valley that stood squarely in the way when there was no business to be gained? The route from the Rogue River was nearly a straight line all the way to Ashland. Railroad engineers love to build straight-line track for their work goes faster, it is easier, and it costs less.

There was also the rudimentary matter of how much would

it cost to fuel a locomotive to haul cars from the Rogue River to Jacksonville should a track be put there? When Lt. Abbot stopped at Fort Lane, he determined the elevation at the fort, along side which the track was proposed, was 1,202 feet.

(As the crow flies to Jacksonville from Fort Lane, about twelve miles, winding through the hills would be a little farther. Jacksonville is 1,569 feet elevation. Jacksonville was 367 feet higher / 12 miles (30.5 ft. / mile). The Medford benchmark reads 1,383 feet elevation, an increase of 181 feet for about the same distance (15 ft. / mile) – half as steep. The straight-line following Bear Creek would take less fuel, less water = lower operating costs. But this is hind-sight.)

Mary Phipps, daughter of land owner Ira J. Phipps, used a pencil on sheets of tablet paper to write:

The surveyors first ran a line out probably a mile west of the present R.R. The next line ran about parallel with Central Avenue but it ran right thru [*sic*] the cemetery at Phoenix [four-plus miles south of Medford] so they shifted it to the present location.

The land owners of Central Point immediately began to raise objections to giving right-of-way and the R.R. had to force the right-of-way.

The R. R. officials came to my father, I. J. Phipps, and asked what he was going to charge for a right-of-way. He answered: "Whatever you think it is worth. They took 120 feet a mile long and paid him less than $100.00.

The next move was to locate the town. The man who had that in charge told my father that he wanted to locate a town and he said all he would ask was every other block. He also assured him that the town would prosper because of his fair [*sic*] treatment of the R.R.

The Phipps acreage was north of Main [Street] extending one mile and containing 120 acres. South side was owned by J. W. Broback. The west portion by Beekman Banker of Jacksonville.

> **Mary Phipps' statement, which she titled, "Locating of Medford," stops, and is here faithfully transcribed, with no mention of the fourth landowner, Mingus.**

Ruby Hiatt wrote a paper for a history class at Southern Oregon College in 1957. The paper was to show property affected by an agreement made October 27, 1883 between P. P. Prim and the Oregon & California Railroad Company as to how the property was distributed and how the results of the transaction would become the basis for the founding of the City of Medford.

The O. & C. wanted to build a town at the middle ford of Bear Creek which is almost in the center of the valley. The area desired was owned by four parties:

C. C. Beekman   C. Mingus
C. W. Broback   I. J. Phipps

There four, with Prim as their trustee, drew an agreement wherein they deeded two hundred forty acres (240) to a trustee designated by the O. & C. The trustee was Davis Loring. Prim and Loring, working with those whom they represented, worked out a comprehensive property agreement.

Loring would receive a free and clear title to two hundred forty (240) acres as designated in the contact, providing he met some requirements. His responsibility was, as a professional engineer for the O. & C., as well as trustee for this deal, to survey, layout and establish a townsite. When the work was completed, he would deed the acreage back to Prim who in turn would deed it, according to the agreement, to the four original property owners, O. & C. and to the Oregon and Transcontinental Railroad Company (O. & T.), lessee of O. & C.

> **Observers have noted the railroad never planned to pass through Jacksonville all the way back to the very earliest planning stages – that 1855 survey by the United States Army Corps of Topographical Engineers.**

The first winter the townsite was dedicated, 1883-1884, the railroad was built as far as Phoenix. This was about five miles southeast of Medford. By April of 1884, there were about forty buildings in Medford and many tents. Quite a number of merchants in Jacksonville put up buildings to serve as "warehouses" near the railroad, and some merchants just closed in Jacksonville and moved to be near where the new action was located.

Medford grew so rapidly that immediate steps to incorporate were taken and on February 24, 1885, Governor Z. F. Moody signed the papers of incorporation. Broback was one who did not want to see a formal city and its government. He became pretty upset when the telegram notifying the people of the city's incorporation was posted in a store window.

On March 11, 1885, an election took place to adopt corpor-

The plaque is not dated but was placed by the Southern Oregon Historical Society in 1983 on the track side of the railroad depot. It was later moved to Alba Park. For a picture, please turn to the "About the Authors" page in the back of this book.

ate papers and to elect trustees for the new city. Medford's first Board of Trustees included J. S. Howard, I. J. Phipps, A. Childers and E. P. Geary. Howard was elected President of the Board.

The question comes up:

Who Started or Founded Medford?

The answer, as we have seen, must be that the city was founded by a "committee" of the four principal land owners, the two trustees Prim and Loring and the O. & C., Railroad.

Recalling, from the map, that both Phipps' and Broback's residential property was inside the original line drawn for the townsite, these properties were declared exempt – "county" – and not included in the "city limits." Therefore when Howard built his house, his was the first home built in Medford.

It is interesting to observe that although Phipps did not live within the city limits, he was one of the first elected to the Board of Trustees of the city.

Storekeepers in Jacksonville were getting nervous about construction at the new town. Some told customers the building projects there were warehouses for transfer of goods from the railroad to Jacksonville. After all, Jacksonville *is* the county seat and as such, *is* the center of county operations. The new court house would be built the next year and that alone meant stability, they truly believed.

Meanwhile, and very quietly, some J-ville, merchants prepared to move to the new town, "Medford," as the place was being called. The town had been founded – platted – during December 1883. It was a little over one year later, February 24, 1885 to be exact, when Governor Z. F. Moody signed the bill incorporating the City of Medford. On March 11, 1885, articles of incorporation were locally adopted.

Jacksonville began to feel it was slipping, when word first got out that the railroad would miss town. Many shook their heads in wonder as to their future as Medford, that upstart railroad town to the east, became a reality. But "li'l old 'J'ville" would survive as a one-industry town – the county seat –another 44 years. When the politicians started to promote the removal of the county seat to Medford in the 1920's, Jacksonville's future took on the look of a freight train roaring down hill without any brakes. *

Railroad promoters and the politicians never seemed to give up. A grandiose plan was to hook on to the transcontinental line at Winnemucca, Nevada, cross the mountains into Oregon and into the Willamette Valley with the western terminal at Newport on the coast. This was called the "Winnemucca-to-the-Sea" concept.** Although the promoters' scheme was not well received in Oregon, and was dropped, another was hatched. As the rails neared Eugene, a plan was to follow Lt. Williamson's original survey by running the track into Central Oregon by way of the middle fork of the Willamette River. This would pass through the towns of Lowell and Oakridge to Chemult then south to Klamath Falls and onward into California.

---

* For the story Jacksonville, refer to *Jacksonville Oregon, Antique Town in a Modern Age.* Jacksonvillians got their railroad but had to built it themselves. For the colorful story about this, refer to *Single Track to Jacksonville* in bibliography.

** One route west from Winnemucca may have been to follow the Applegate Trail of 1846. This route passed through the Black Rock Desert and the amazing High Rock Canyon through the Sierra-Nevada Mountains in northwest Nevada, Fandango Pass in northeast California, then enter Oregon near Klamath Falls. For description and pictures of the route refer to *Over the Applegate Trail to Oregon in 1846* in bibliography.

(This route was eventually accepted as an alternate as the line over the Siskiyou Mountains, at the south end of the Rogue River Valley, had extremely high operating costs and the steepest track on the entire Southern Pacific line – 3.3%. In 1985, AMTRAK passenger service between Portland and San Francisco adopted the Willamette River - Central Oregon route – called the Natron cutoff – bypassing all the cities in western Oregon south of Eugene. See map on page 26.)

Getting a railroad, any railroad, from Portland to Medford and south, was a political and entrepreneureal challenge.

Had it not been for Senator Williams and the assertiveness, aggressiveness and brashness of Southern Oregonians who bellowed their demands for the route to California by way of Southern Oregon, some historians believe the Rogue Valley would not have received rails at all. These people would have no part of a deal with the Winnemucca-by-the-sea promotion and assertively shouted down the plan to run the rail line into Central Oregon out of Eugene.

Henry Villard came into control of the Oregon and California Railroad through a succession of financial deals and personages that included Ben Holladay. Ben Holladay is important in Oregon rail history as it was he who got construction going at Portland in 1868. By 1873, his trains were rolling into Roseburg but there they ground to a stop for nearly ten years. This is attributed, by many historians, to the national financial panic of that year and what some call the mishandling by Holladay.

Three years later, Villard came on the scene. In super-colossal deals, that included taking over where Holladay had stopped, and involved other railroads and steamship interests that gave Wall Street financiers the "willies." Villard put together his package to push rails out of Roseburg to the California line.

Villard ordered surveyors into the field but, owing to the extraordinary challenge of trying to get through the Calapooya Mountains in winter, he accomplished only sixty miles graded during 1881-1882. He would not have his route finalized to the border until the summer of 1883.

(Villard's engineers rejected Lt. Abbot's 1855 route up the Canyon Creek canyon (today's Interstate-5) south of Canyonville, in favor of a route up Cow Creek canyon to Glendale. This is the only detour from the 1855 survey in Western Oregon, other than a slight re-aligning in the Siskiyou Mountains.)

Villard addressed the Portland Board of Trade:

> The Oregon and California Company gave me more trouble than any other of my enterprises. This continued throughout my connection of nearly twelve years with that ill-fated concern.... The proceeds from new bonds remaining after paying off a mortgage lien [elsewhere] proved upon the final location of the Siskiyou line to fall short nearly $2,000,000 of the total required to ... the junction with the Central Pacific [in California]. This was dreadful ... threatening the company with the fatal calamity of having to stop work and consequent dead waste of millions [already] spent on grading, bridging and tunnels. [Our funds] were exhausted in January 1883 but we managed to continue work till spring.

Finally, a scheme evolved for a new firm, the Oregon & Transportation Company, and the O. & C., whereby the O. & T. would finish construction then lease the finished road back to the O. & C.

By May 17, 1892, O. & T. had sold most of its property in the city. That which remained, was, on that day, sold to George H. Andrews of Portland, in a transaction that bought up all O. & T. interests in Grants Pass, Dardenelles (across the river from

---

John S. Howard:

He was the first mayor as one might call the former "President of the Board of Trustees."

He was Medford's first postmaster. His "post office" was a cigar box in which he collected outgoing mail and stashed incoming mail for the local folks to stop by his store to pick it up.

He was also Trustee for the O. & T.'s forty-one blocks of city property.

He was the Medford agent for Wells Fargo Express.

He built the first store building, having opened for business in a tent, and he operated that store as the first proprietor of a retail establishment in Medford.

He was the surveyor for the railroad.

Mr. John S. Howard was a very busy and important personage in the new City of Medford.

The Phipps residence was within the new city limits but it was declared exempt from taxes. The property is about where today's Greyhound bus depot is located (LOWER) at 5th and Bartlett Streets.

Gold Hill), Central Point, Phoenix, and Ashland. Andrews was secretary-treasurer of the Southern Pacific Company that took over the management and operations of the O. & C. Railroad on July 1, 1887. In addition, Andrews was a director of several other companies active in transportation. He was reportedly a close associate of Henry Villard.

The land, city blocks and lots acquired by Andrews for the

Waverly Cottage was built in 1898 and is today a Bed & Breakfast. It is listed on the _National Register of Historic Places_ and is located at N. Grape and 4th Streets.

Southern Pacific were largely sold a little at a time. But after 1955, when passenger service through the Rogue River Valley was terminated, many lots were sold to major Medford businesses after the passenger station and ramps were demolished. (The first passenger station had been located in the middle of what is now Main Street, a severe obstruction to traffic, on the east side of the track.) The Jackson County Federal Savings and Loan Association, which established in 1909, (was acquired recently by Key Bank of Oregon) put up a major building, on the south side of Main Street, as did First Intestate Bank (now Wells Fargo Bank) on the north side of Main Street (originally designated as 7th Street), all former S. P. property. Even so, quite a bit of property, including switching facilities and rights-of-way through the city remain. These facilities are owned by Rail-Tex (of Texas) on which it operates the Central Oregon and Pacific Railroad – S.P. having sold its interests south of Eugene in 1995. The freight station still stands, but at this writing is planned for conversion to a non-railroad oriented business. ⬦

2

An Era of Trolley Cars

Hundreds of cities and towns across America had a fling with electric street railways and Medford was one of them. Some of these street car lines are still in business but most are long-gone, and in some cases records about them are difficult to locate. Medford is one of the latter.

The authors quickly learned there are no city maps showing the tracks, as tracks are considered "street improvements" and not necessarily permanent. But some of Medford's rails are still in place, very "permanent," buried under the asphalt.

It should be pointed out, to avoid confusion, that there were two rail systems for passengers, on Medford streets. The earliest was a steam train. This was the Rogue River Valley Railroad, a short-line that ran between Medford and Jacksonville. This line was the outgrowth of the fact that the mainline railroad did not go through Jacksonville. The folks there wanted a railroad so badly they built their own. The east terminal for the line was in down town Medford, in the vicinity of the Southern Pacific station. The little Porter locomotive chugged along Eighth Street pulling just a single passenger car. *

The other passenger rail system on Medford streets was the Southern Oregon Traction Company. It was organized on July 15, 1913 and obtained a franchise from the city to run an electric car for transporting the public on the city streets. Spencer S. Bullis was the entrepreneur in the venture. Earlier, he had operated street cars in Mississippi. His intention was to install a line on the Medford streets then join with the stream train interurban that operated into Jacksonville after electrifying the latter. For power, Bullis had a contract with the California-Oregon Power Company (COPCO). His dream included interurban extensions to Ashland with stops in Phoenix and Talent, then north four miles to Central Point. But these lines never materialized.

He installed a single track from the east side of the Southern

---

* For the amazing history of the Jacksonville railroad, refer to *Single Track to Jacksonville*, in bibliography.

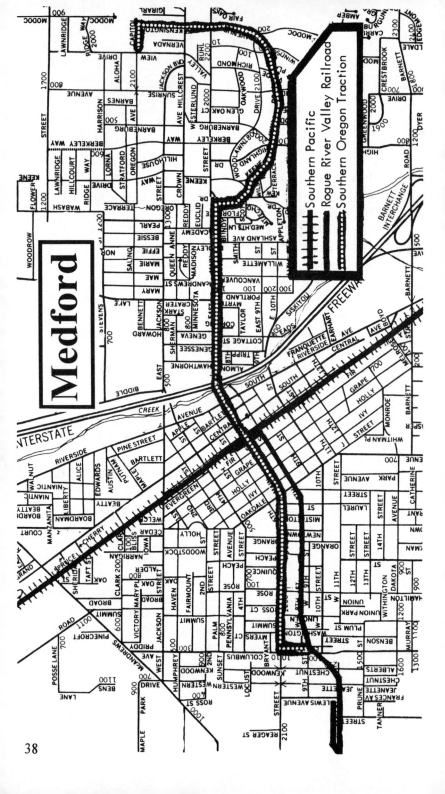

Medford

Southern Pacific
Rogue River Valley Railroad
Southern Oregon Traction

38

Locomotive of the Rogue River Valley Railroad, the "Jacksonville line," with steam up, seems about ready to roll for Jacksonville. This is at the temporary depot (tent, at right) when the system was new. Woman seems to be headed for the train while man (inset) is running to get aboard. A close look reveals that while the car was connected to the locomotive, the hose for the air brake on the car appears to be dangling. Camera faces east on Main Street, which is blocked by the passenger car. Train faces south on Evergreen Street but that street has never been developed to the present time.

Section gang installs track for Medford's trolley line on West Main Street between Holly and Ivy with a steam locomotive rented from the Rogue River Valley Railroad for the job. In March 1985, when a crew was digging to install underground conduit for computer-controlled traffic signals, their tools hit the rails, which had been paved over after the streetcar line went out of business. When rail was removed from around town on various projects, top priorities for disposition of its pieces went to researchers and museums.

Pacific track on Main Street, crossed Bear Creek and ran east to about today's Eastwood Drive. Later the line was extended south on Eastwood to Keene Way thence around the circular Keene Way Drive to Modoc. This route avoided climbing Medford's steep "east" hill. In attempting to trace the route today, one must keep in mind that most of this area was vacant with few dedicated streets and even fewer houses. His track ran north on Modoc Avenue, crossed Main and Hillcrest to Capitol where it turned west alongside the city reservoir. The end of the track was about one block from the present Valley View Drive.

Poles that supported the catenary (overhead wire) for the trolley are placed opposite each other. The authors, along with the late M. Dale Newton, railroad historian, discovered what are believed to be two sets of these poles. Both are on Modoc Avenue. One set is immediately south of East Main Street and the other set is just north of East Main Street.

As we have noted, Bullis' route skirted the steep East Main Street hill (today's major east-west route through this part of Medford). Some claim the street cars stopped in front of Sacred Heart Hospital which was atop a bluff near the end of the present Medford Heights Lane. But "in front" probably meant about a block or so down the hill from the door on either Eastwood Drive or the East Main Street sides.

Early residents of the area told the authors that "the streets weren't paved up this way then. The car track was on ties just sitting in the dirt."

David L. Stearns, another late rail historian, wrote in 1955 about the trolleys:

The day I was there in August 1914, the temperature was about 105 degrees. Mr. Hall, proprietor of a garage back of the Medford Hotel, took us for an afternoon ride around the valley to attempt to cool us off. That evening, after dark, I recall [some] things about that [trolley] line. It ran precisely at the S.P. crossing on Main Street (the car laid over there between runs). It ran east on Main Street to the foot of the hill then ran along the base of the bench below the Catholic hospital. The line had many curves beyond the hospital and that nice, new, single trucker [Brill car] jerked in rounding them.

I recall we passed a brightly lighted building close to the track on our right and was told that was the club house of the Medford Golf Course.

Somewhere out in the Heights district, the line turned north then west and ended at the east side of a knoll crowned by a reservoir. The motorman urged

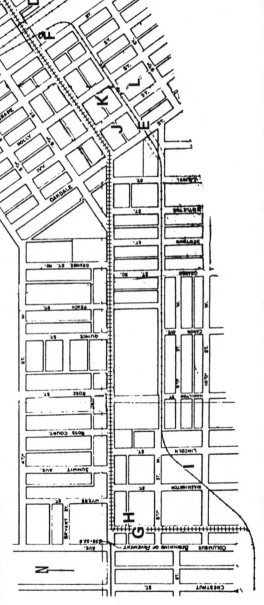

Medford – Central Area

Identification of symbols: *A-* East end of track after removal of Siskiyou Heights extension; *B-* Bear Creek; *C-* S.P. main line track; *D-* S.P. passenger depot; *E-* Rogue River Valley RR on 8th Street; *F-* RRVR depot; *G-* Trolley line extended to join RVRR track after steam service discontinued; *H-* Highland Park trolley layover (parking) site; *I-* Line of poplar trees parallel to abandoned rail line near West 9th and Lincoln Streets; *J-* Public Library; *K-* Alba Park *L-* Post Office.

The Southern Oregon Traction Company cars were adapted for 1-man operation which meant that the Operator was both Motorman and Conductor. Shown is Ray Blackburn, the Operator. Destination sign above window reads EAST MAIN.

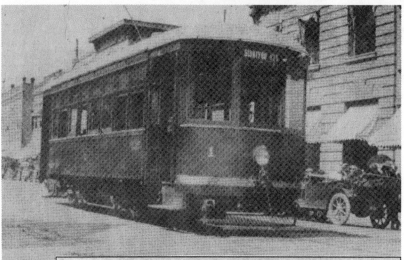

Screened old classic portrait of Brill-Birney trolley car No. 1 on Medford's East Main Street. The destination sign indicates the car was headed for SISKIYOU HTS (Siskiyou Heights).

us to walk up to and around the reservoir for a view out over the valley. We did so and when we had changed ends [to operate the trolley from the other end to go back into town], he joined us and spent some time pointing out the sights to us.

On the return trip, the car stopped near the Golf Club sort of automatically. I suppose it was about 8 or 9 o'clock); the lights inside the building were turned out one-by-one and then the building was all dark. We just sat there. Soon a man emerged from the darkness and boarded the trolley.

We had been the only passengers on the car during the out-bound trip and had become quite chummy with the motorman, and he introduced the new passenger as the pro at the Gold Club.

In view of the leisurely nature of the trip we took that evening, I assume the line had about an hourly schedule at that time of day.

Bullis had been convinced by real estate promoters to extend his line into the Siskiyou Heights development (the east hill), as developers were certain his trolley would reap rich rewards from all the folks who lived up there and who needed to go to town. But the development was much slower than forecast. The trolley line was losing money and Bullis was looking for a way out.

After the fad of riding on a new street car had worn off, the car was usually running pretty empty. Spencer Bullis had carried 20,000 riders his first year at 5¢ each. But he determined that the Siskiyou Heights extension was not a profitable end of town to have his terminal.

As we have seen, his track stopped just short of crossing the

(TOP) The Operator stopped his car and alighted for this picture. Car is headed *west* on Main Street although destination sign car reads EAST MAIN. This is a Brill-Birney single-truck, double-ender with a trolley *wheel* running along the catenary. Most later models used a "shoe" or "scraper" on the wire. Some sources claim that Bullis bought two of these cars from Portland, Oregon. (LOWER) These cars could seat about 28 people. After the fad of riding the "new" trolley wore off, the cars seldom hauled more than a handful at a time.

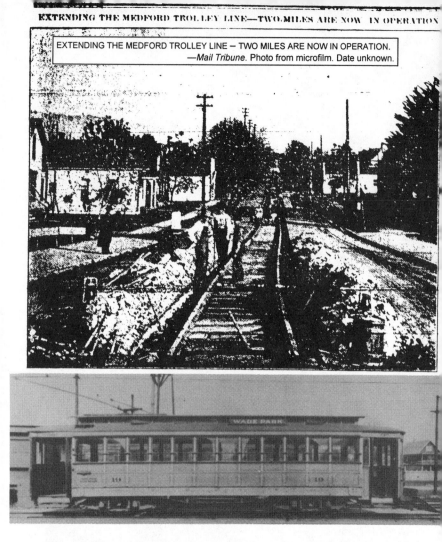

EXTENDING THE MEDFORD TROLLEY LINE – TWO MILES ARE NOW IN OPERATION.
—*Mail Tribune*. Photo from microfilm. Date unknown.

When Bullis obtained operating rights to Jacksonville, he realized that the little 28-passenger Brill-Birney cars could not carry the anticipated passenger load. He purchased a used Kuhlman double truck car in Cleveland, Ohio. The car had to be converted to a double-ender and a second trolley (not shown in the photo which was made in Cleveland before the deal). Unfortunately, this seems to be the only picture of this car other than the view of it (page 47) after it was abandoned. Not only did this top-of-the-line 1902 car run on the country line to Jacksonville, it ran on Medford's Main Street to the end of the line between Riverside and Bear Creek.

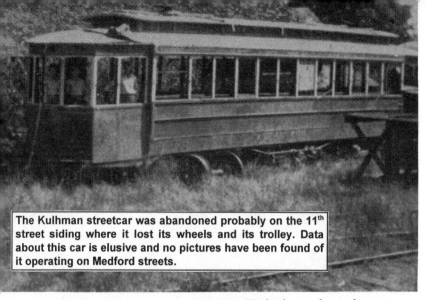

The Kulhman streetcar was abandoned probably on the 11th street siding where it lost its wheels and its trolley. Data about this car is elusive and no pictures have been found of it operating on Medford streets.

Southern Pacific rails on Main Street. He had not planned to terminate there but much delay was encountered getting "crossing frogs" for his track as well as an agreement with S. P. to cross their line. It was probably largely a matter of money for S.P. was not about to dig up and break its main line rails for the benefit of a street car unless somebody – Bullis – paid for it and in advance.

Eventually the work was done and the trolley line continued west on Main to about Oakdale. It's most important little piece of business was hauling visitors from the train depot up the street to the Medford Hotel. It was just a few blocks, but with heavy luggage, the 5¢ fare was much less than a taxi. While no records have been found to establish it as fact, evidence indicates the trolley was conveniently on the west side at the S.P. crossing when the passenger trains stopped. As the trolley was a "double-ender" – could be operated from either end, and there was only the single track in the middle of the street, it was no big deal to go back and forth just between the depot and the hotel if need be.

Such was the case when a visiting school band and basketball team came to town and had rented a number of rooms at the hotel. The little trolley shuttled between the two points until all the adults were transferred to the hotel. The teen-age musicians and ball players had to walk unless then had the nickel fare.

Forlorn, early morning on a winter day with a lonely streetcar on West Main Street in Medford. Hotel Medford on right.

Later, when Bullis took over the Jacksonville line, he pulled up his track from the east hill and reinstalled the rails out West Main Street to Elm Street. Here he jogged one block to the south (Eighth Street) and switched in to the steam track.

This track started at the Rogue River Valley Railroad's depot which was adjacent from the S. P. station, but on the west side of the S.P. track. The Jacksonville line had track down the center of Eighth Street to about Lincoln where the track veered on about forty-five degrees southwest to Eleventh Street then straightened out for the run to Jacksonville.

SOUTHERN OREGON TRACTION CO.

TIME SCHEDULE NUMBER 2
EFFECTIVE OCTOBER 18, 1916.

Subject to change without notice.

Lv. Jacksonville	Leave Medford end of paving E. Main
7:30 A.M.	8:00 A.M.
8:30 "	9:00 "
9:30 "	10:00 "
10:30 "	11:00 "
11:30 "	12:00 See below.
1:00 P.M.	1:30 P.M.
2:00 "	2:30 "
3:00 "	3:30 "
4:00 "	4:30 "
5:00 "	6:00 "
7:15 "	Leave Riverside Ave.
	10:00 P.M.

The 12:00 car from Medford lays over at Highland Park thirty minutes. Cars pass waiting room going out East Main ten minutes before above schedule and going to Jacksonville eight minutes after.

R.S. BULLIS, Gen'l Pass'r Agt.
Medford, Ore.

SOUTHERN OREGON TRACTION CO.

EFFECTIVE JUNE 1, 1917.

Subject to change without notice.

Lv. Jacksonville	Leave Medford
7:30 A.M.	8:00 A.M.
8:30 "	9:00 "
9:30 "	10:00 "
10:30 "	11:00 "
11:30 "	12:00 NOON
1:00 P.M.	1:30 P.M.
2:00 "	2:30 "
3:00 "	3:30 "
4:00 "	4:30 "
5:00 "	6:00 "
7:30 "	10:00 "

R.S. BULLIS,
Gen. Freight & Passenger Agent

SOUTHERN OREGON TRACTION CO.

TIME TABLE No. 5
EFFECTIVE AUGUST 23, 1917.
Subject to change without notice.

Lv. Jacksonville	Leave Medford
7:30 A.M. daily except Sunday	8:00 A.M. daily except Sunday
7:50 A.M. Sunday only	8:30 A.M. Sunday only
8:30 A.M. daily except Sunday	9:00 A.M. daily except Sunday
9:00 A.M. Sunday only	10:00 A.M. daily
9:30 A.M. except Sunday	12:00 Noon-daily except Sunday
11:30 A.M. daily except Sunday	2:30 P.M. daily
2:00 P.M. daily	3:30 P.M. daily
3:00 P.M. daily	4:30 P.M. daily
4:00 P.M. daily	6:00 P.M. daily
5:00 P.M. daily (Note 1)	10:00 P.M. daily
7:15 P.M. daily (Note 2)	

R.S. BULLIS,
Gen. Freight & Passenger Agent

SOUTHERN OREGON TRACTION CO.

TIME TABLE
EFFECTIVE FEBRUARY 23, 1919.
Subject to change without notice.

Lv. Jacksonville	Leave Medford
7:20 A.M. daily except Sunday	8:00 A.M. daily except Sunday
8:30 A.M. daily except Sunday	9:30 A.M. Sunday only
10:00 A.M. Sunday only	9:45 A.M. daily except Sunday
11:30 A.M. daily except Sunday	10:38 A.M. Sunday only
2:00 P.M. daily	12:08 Noon-daily
3:45 P.M. daily	2:45 P.M. daily
5:00 P.M. daily	4:30 P.M. daily
7:15 P.M. Wed. & Sat. only	6:09 P.M. daily
	10:00 P.M. Wed. & Sat. only

R.S. BULLIS,
Gen. Freight & Passenger Agent

There are very few surviving Time Tables. From them one can observe the changing schedules and the cutback in service toward the end of the operation.

Streetcar, Yes – Interurban, No.

Southern Oregon Traction Company was never an official "interurban," according to the classic definition on an interurban line just because it used the rails that joined Jacksonville and Medford. For all practical purposes, SOTCO remained a street traction company merely with an extended line into the country.

But there were true "interurban" railways in Oregon and elsewhere using heavy-duty cars on short mileage runs, but those short hauls were often parts of greater inter-city systems. In Portland, an "interurban" ran the 25 miles to Oregon City. The Sausalito - Mill Valley line in California, just north of San Francisco, and the Medford - Jacksonville line were the same length – 6 miles. This Mill Valley line was part of the Northwestern Pacific, a true interurban, which had half-a-dozen routes extending from the Sausalito ferry dock to points about 25 miles away.

The Market Street Railway Company in San Francisco, with hundreds of miles of track in the city, had a similar situation as the Jacksonville line. MSRY's San Mateo run was only an "extended line into the country" even though the distance was about 20 miles between terminals. This line (No. 40), ran ordinary streetcar equipment on this rural line as did the Southern Oregon Traction Company.

A little west of Columbus Avenue, at about Jeanette Street, and parallel to the unpaved Eleventh Street (Meadows Lane), a spur was added earlier to serve a small lumber mill. After the mill closed, the track remained. Years later the once attractive Kuhlman double-truck trolley car was abandoned on that spur as shown in our picture.

After Spencer Bullis reclaimed his rails from the east hill of Medford, his eastern terminal was at Eastwood Drive. One might ride "straight through" from Eastwood Drive into down town Jacksonville for a single fare. When occasional freight needed hauling between the towns, he got out a steam engine to pull a freight car. Freight continued to be run on the original Eighth Street line to the S.P. track, where there was a switch allowing through freight cars for Jacksonville. These were easily switched from the main line onto the interurban track. Until

Note: Although numerous people have tried to locate the power company sub-station that fed the trolley wire, no exact place has been found. David L. Stearns' map shows Highland Park about 2 + miles west of Jacksonville but the track west of Jacksonville was never electrified. Others point to topographic map coordinates that translate into a plot in Jacksonville on N. Oregon Street about 1 block from the depot. This is plausible. Still others, including Dr. William L. Barnum, told the authors, "the sub-station was at Highland Park in *Medford*." From an electrical engineering standpoint, this is the most logical location as the feed to the catenary, about in the middle of the length of the line, would best serve the need.

Driving and Stopping a Streetcar

The Controller (handle at left) is in OFF position. When the Motorman slowly twists the handle clockwise, one click-stop at a time, the car starts and picks up speed. With the handle advanced all the way around the circle to the stud, this gives full speed on level track. A Brill-Birney car would do up to about 30 mph. The Kuhlman could do about 50 mph if it did not have a governor.

The handle to the right is the direction switch. In the position shown, the car could be moved FORWARD. When this wrench-like handle is pulled clockwise to the stud, the car could be moved backward. Whenever a Motorman left his car, he was to always take this wrench with him so no one could move his streetcar.

Handle at far right operates the airbrake. In position shown, brake is off. In inset, brake is on. Air brake operation required a skilled Motorman to keep the car from jerking and risk throwing the passengers out of their seats. A pressure gauge was on every streetcar so the Motorman would know he had "air" and could stop the streetcar. Gauge is "0" as the car was not in operation.

—Photographed at National Seashore Trolley Museum, Kennebunkport, Maine by authors.
For more information on streetcars, refer to *Single Track to Jacksonville* in bibliography.

51

"Car Tickets"

"Commute" tickets were sold 20 in a book. Although tickets were "not good if detached," most parents broke up a book and spread the tickets around the family or among fellow workers on the job. Streetcar operators didn't seem to mind. But once punched –"validated"– by the Conductor, a ticket could not be reused. The idea behind the tickets was to reward steady riders with a 10% discount.

Ticket books also brought larger unit sales to the streetcar companies and many people never used all the tickets or lost their books. Unused tickets translated into unearned profits for the line.

early 1996, the original switch between the lines was still in use, but the Jacksonville track had been terminated on the north side of Sixth Street for decades. This spur was called a "caboose" parking track, but the authors more often saw diesel locomotives parked there. That switch and the spur are now gone.

It seems whenever something good comes along, there are those who try to offer a "like" product or service for less money – cheaper most call it. During the heyday of interurban lines and street car services in many cities, jitney drivers were assertively hawking business and could leave either Jacksonville or Medford on a non-scheduled basis. But the train, and later the trolley on the "Jville" line had to maintain a published schedule. If Bullis was to hold on to his passengers, he would have to compete and that he did by cutting his fares. He regularly operated eight round trips each day with the steam train and announced he would continue eight trips as quickly as the Jacksonville line was electrified.

The first use of the name, "Southern Oregon Traction Company," referring to the entire line extending from downtown Medford to Jacksonville, was in a advertisement in the Medford *Sun* on November 27, 1915.

A second light-weight Brill trolley car was brought in, plus a double-truck, double-ended full-size Kuhlman street car. Now the line had three trolleys with which to do business. And business was good – for awhile. In 1916, according to stories in the Medford *Sun*, the citizens of Medford voted favorably for municipal bonds to pay for construction of a city railway to reach as far as thirty miles west of Jacksonville. There were supposed to be mineral and timber resources just waiting to be tapped and of course, real estate promoters hooted the advantages of living in this extended suburb. Bullis, the owner and operator of the trolley line, wanted to build such a railroad but very quickly pulled in his horns.

Although he was profiting nicely from the daily street car business, the high interest he had to pay on his debt along with the burden of a new city contact, forced him into bankruptcy. Passenger service came to an end as swiftly as turning off the power switch, which the power company promptly did.

The Line of Trees – Reminder of a Railroad

Today, one standing on the southeast corner of Eighth and Lincoln in front of the Fire Station and looking to the southwest, will first observe the slightly leaning evergreen tree in the yard on the Lincoln Street side of the Fire House. Next, sight in a southwesterly direction and locate the row of ancient trees – five of them at this writing – cutting diagonally across a residential yard. These trees are the remainder of a long line of trees that had been planted along the south side of the railroad.

After the rails were taken up, many dozens of lengths were far too worn for use ever again on a railroad, were requisitioned by the Medford Street Department. For many years one could find these rails used for sign posts at street crossings. In recent years, most have been pulled up and replaced with "break-away" posts.

One of his little Brill single-truck trolleys had a burned out motor. With only one motor available, the car could be shunted here and there, slowly, but without any weight of passengers. It was parked on the west end spur off Jeanette Street. The other Brill was apparently run off the track and parked in the dirt near Bear Creek near main Street. The Kuhlman car also went to the

Commuter bus of the 1920's (TOP) **runs on unpaved highway 99 between Medford and Ashland. Fuel was an unleaded distillate called "white" gasoline.**
(— photo from RVTD)
Modern natural-gas burning commuter bus of 1996 (LOWER) **at Medford Bus Transfer Station of Rogue Valley Transportation District.**   —Bert Webber photo

During one period, there were commuter gasoline-powered Mc Keen "wind-splitters" operated by Southern Pacific. These popular single-car "trains" ran between Ashland and Grants Pass with stops along the way including Medford. Three of the sharp-nosed cars, hence the term "wind-splitters," were Number 9 (71 seats), No. 55 (75 seats), No. 63 (62 seats). These heavy steel cars were up to seventy feet long. They cruised up to 50 miles per hour with their 200 horsepower truck engines. The last McKeen in the U.S. was retired in 1950. There is currently a move to convince the Central Oregon & Pacific Railroad, successor to S.P., to run commuter trains between Yreka and Grants Pass.

storage track off Jeanette. The big car, with its wheels and motors removed, was vandalized over the years and a single report indicates what was left of it went to a World War-II scrap metal drive.

The single track in the center of Main Street and in the center of Eighth Street, is mostly still there but is paved over. In September of 1981, efforts were made to remove the old rails from the deteriorating Main Street Bridge to lighten the loan on the bridge. Under the blacktop, engineers discovered the bases of the rails were permanently embedded in concrete. Even through only the tops of the rails could be removed with cutting torches, the weight on the old bridge was considerably lessened.

At the present time passengers are transported throughout Medford, and the surrounding areas, by the Rogue Valley Transportation District. This is a system of busses with several being new models that burn natural gas instead of gasoline or diesel oil. Where Bullis once imagined a line from Ashland through Medford and extending to Central Point, the RVTD busses now make these runs every day. ◇

3

Medford's Architect
Frank C. Clark

Frank Chamberlain Clark
(1872-1957)

Frank Clark was Medford's first registered architect and lived and worked in the Rogue River Valley from 1903 until he died in 1957 at the age of 85. He worked alone (except for a short time in 1911), until 1937 when a professional association with another architect, Robert J. Keeney, started.

During his lifetime, he designed commercial and residential buildings with the majority of them in Medford. Born in 1872 in New York, he studied at Cooper Union and apprenticed himself to distinguished architects among them Oscar S. Teale, Arthur Curtis Longyear and Robert Gibson. Before starting his own office, he worked with McKim, Mead and White in New York

This school started its existence as Medford High School, later was changed to a Junior High and presently it serves as McLoughlin Middle School. It is located at 320 West 2nd Street, Medford.

The fateful night "8888" (August 8, 1988) when the Medford Hotel, a local landmark for generations, was totally destroyed by fire. But the original Frank Clark drawings were available so the hotel was rebuilt to original specifications (ABOVE) as shown in 1996.

Frank Clark designed hundreds of private residences as well as many commercial and institutional buildings. Those homes shown here are merely representative. (LOWER) The palatial residence known as the Edgar Hafer House (1905) was remodled to become the Perl Funeral Parlor about 1908 and still serves in that role.

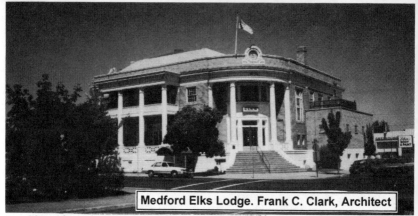

Medford Elks Lodge. Frank C. Clark, Architect

City where he became polished in his profession.

At just 24 years old, young Clark abandoned New York for Los Angeles. This was in 1896. In southern California he went to work for Frederick Roehrig where he remained just two years before moving into Arizona to work for Ezra Bartlett who was doing work in Jerome and Prescott. By age 31, Frank Clark pulled out of the southland and moved to Ashland, Oregon. In Ashland, he designed the gymnasium then finished a design for the Administration Building of the state normal school.

Frank Clark enjoyed Southern Oregon and except for the 1907-1908 year, he spent his life there. He took Frank S. Forster as a partner for a short time in 1911, then in 1937, at age 65, he associated, until his death, with Robert Keeney.

Clark did not limit his design work to commercial buildings of residences, but undertook whatever the community required. He was the architect for schools, civic buildings, lodge halls, warehouses, an airport administration building and hangar, stadium bleachers sports, a rural orchardist's complex, and anything else what was sought.

He was the prime architect of his time in southern Oregon and particularly in Medford. A number of his monuments (buildings) are listed in the *National Register of Historic Places.*

Of the 35 Institutions designed by Frank Clark, just 18 remain. Schools and churches seem to have a greater survival rate. Three of four churches he designed stand today and half the fraternal buildings remain. In Medford, there are seven schools standing. As for churches, examples of his work stand in Medford, Central Point and Ashland.

As no complete list of Frank C. Clark buildings has hereto-

Frank Clark designed the addition to Roosevelt School in Medford (TOP) and the Manager's Residence (LOWER) and other structures, at Hillcrest Orchards east of Medford.

fore been made available in a popular book, the publisher is listing all known Clark designed buildings in the Appendix of this book. This is, of course, a working list and is subject to change. ◇

4

Medford's Medical Might

There are two major factors that developed over the years to establish Medford as the largest medical center between Portland and San Francisco.

1) A tremendous growth that occurred within the city and extended areas that was large enough to support two small hospitals. This population growth continues to the present time.

2) A large number and wide variety of specialties among physicians especially following World War-II. These numbers and specialties continue to grow.

Medford's first hospital was located on the southwest corner of W. Main and 11th Streets and opened with the name Southern Oregon Hospital in 1906. This hospital had 14 beds. Prior to that time, sick patients were usually treated in their own beds at their homes with the doctors making "house calls."

By 1910, several doctors formed a committee and petitioned the Sisters of Charity of Providence in Portland to start a hospital in Medford. Following a short inquiry, this Order bought the Southern Oregon Hospital. The first three nuns – administrator - nurses – arrived on May 27, 1911. On that day, the hospital was full – fourteen patients and seven nurses.

This morning we directed our steps toward the hospital full of courage [and] started our day's work. The nurses were leaving the same day so we took the entire administration of the establishment and if its patients.

—Sister Pascal. May 27, 1911

Today we are meeting a good number of the doctors. Some wish us well and say they are happy to have us, some are cold and barely looked at us.

—Sister Pascal. May 28, 1911

One of the first moves of the nuns was to discontinue the name "Southern Oregon Hospital" and start their work under the name "Sacred Heart Hospital."

The preparations for the construction on what became the new Sacred Heart Hospital were under way within one week! This was a tall building of five stories. Tall, because the rooms had 12-foot ceilings. It was built of brick and stood on Siskiyou Heights then called "Nob Hill."

The nuns, looking forward to occupying the entire fourth floor as their home, with a chapel, called the hospital "our beautiful red brick castle." (—Sister Pascal Dec. 27, 1911)

In a speech on Consecration Day, February 18, 1912, the hospital was declared to be "the most modern hospital west of the Mississippi" – indeed, the hospital's owners were proud of their achievement! One of the features was the Department of Roentgenology (X-ray).

Within a few months, money for operating the hospital became very short, and shorter yet was food for the patients and for the nuns.

Our confidence in Divine Providence was being put to the test since we were not even assured of any money for our daily bread. The people have been very generous in sending us fruits and vegetables. A farmer…gave us for our two cows all the hay for the winter season.   —Sister Claire d'Assise, not dated

… Fruit is plentiful and the people are very generous toward us …thirty-five boxes of peaches … fifteen boxes of winter pears … fifty boxes of apples.
—Sister Claire d'Assise, Sept. 20, 1913

Even with shortages, the nuns, reporting on their operations revealed:

1911-1912		1914	
Staff (hospital and church):	12	Staff (hospital and church):	26
Patients: (25 deaths)	301	Patients: (296 free hospitalizations)	392
Paying boarders:	48	Paying boarders:	20
Free meals served to the poor:	350	Free meals served to the poor:	1100

Sacred Heart Hospital cost $125,000 to build and could house up to 125 persons staff and patients (85 beds). The building was five stories with the top floor equipped as surgeries. The building was designed in wings on ground measurements about 115 feet square situated on 2½ acres. Every patient room had exposure for sunlight. There were some private rooms as well as wards, with the largest ward being 20 x 30 feet with 9 beds. The landscaped grounds had walkways and numerous benches where ambulatory patients in summer could go to sit. The trolley car (fare 5¢) that ran to downtown Medford (Southern Oregon Traction Company) stopped a block from the hospital.

But all was not peaceful among the public and a number of the physicians in the community because of the Roman Catholic influence at the hospital. Just six years later, Dr. Robert Stearns, MD, opened the Community Hospital in a house at 843 E. Main Street. The need for the non-religious oriented medical facility grew with great rapidity therefore a major building, today's Century Building, was added to the side of the original structure.

(After the hospital vacated the building, its many patient rooms, and other facilities, were converted into office spaces. This building's once having been a hospital is validated by observing that the doors to the offices are extra wide – bed width. It may be noticed that the buildings in the neighborhood of Myrtle Street and E. Main Street, across from the Century Building, resemble doctor's offices, for that is exactly why they were built.)

Community Hospital at 843 E. Main Street. in mid-1950's.

The 59-bed "Community Hospital," as it was called, was officially the Medford Hospital Association. In 1928, two nurses from the mid-west came to town, bought controlling shares and in 1936, they operated the facility.

It was in the late 1940's that a number of people created a fund to buy the nurses' interests. For awhile, the facility was owned by the Protestant Episcopal Church Diocese of Oregon then it again changed legal ownership when it was taken over, in 1954, by a non-profit corporation. During this period it was obvious that the community needed a larger facility. It was attracting patients from a wide area thus the genesis of the idea that Medford become a medical center.

The number of physicians opening offices in Medford was growing sharply. Among the reasons for their arrival was the mild climate and Medford was an escape from large city situations.

It was during this era when Mercy Flights Air Ambulance, (Inc.) was founded as a means of carrying sick Medford people to hospitals elsewhere because of lack of adequate local facilities. (See chapter 11)

The old hospital, now named Century Building, has been converted to offices.

The hospital, if it was to grow beyond the confines of its walls, needed to find new quarters. A gift of half-a-million dollars by Alfred and Helen Bundy Carpenter moved the Board of Directors to find property and build a new hospital. The name was changed to Rogue Valley Memorial Hospital in 1956.

The public donated $900,000 for the hospital. Large private money amounting to $1,309,700 came in. A federal grant of Hill-Burton funds amounting to $564,000 arrived. The Ford Foundation sent $26,300.

With the sum of $2,800.000 on hand or assured, the Board of Directors held a ground-breaking program on the corner of Murphy and Barnett Roads in August 1956. Barely two years later, on May 1, 1958, the new 80-bed hospital opened its doors.

The demand for hospital beds in Medford has seen much growth at this facility:

1958	80	1971 (Includes new Pediatric Pod)	225
1962	160	1978	264
1968	195	1983	293
		1996	305

Rogue Valley Medical Center

In 1984, the name became Rogue Valley Medical Center. In 1996, the hospital became a part of Asante Health Systems. The campus includes a medical emergency helicopter landing pad.

—0—

When the Providence nuns decided to close Sacred Heart Hospital in 1960, due to obsolescence, a number of significant donations persuaded them to keep the old hospital operating until a way to build a new facility could be found. Five years and $2,600,000 later, in spring 1966, the new 93-bed Providence Hospital opened on a campus at McAndrews Road and Crater Lake Avenue. (The old "beautiful red castle," Sacred Heart Hospital was torn down.)

> **Providence Hospital was the first all-private room hospital in the United States.**

Providence Medford Medical Center
(TOP) **Mid-1970's.** (LOWER) **1996**

—Photographs from Providence Medford Medical Center

By 1985, its capacity had been expanded to 168 beds.

Operations at Rogue Valley Medical Center had always included Obstetric and Pediatric Departments, two services that Providence had not offered. But with the trend toward Health Maintenance Organizations (HMO's), an entire maternity department was built, staffed and opened at Providence by January 1, 1995. During that year, the hospital changed its name to Providence Medford Medical Center. This, and other building programs have substantially expanded the hospital's services.

Medford's medical facilities are well in tune to the needs of the ever expanding population growth of the community. ◇

5

Readers, Books and Facilities

The first library in Medford was on some spare shelves in Haskins' Drug Store. This was in 1903 after a number of people in town felt there was a need to have a library. The Medford Library Association was organized on September 25, 1903 with three gentlemen, W. S. Crowell. Dr. Elijah B. Pickel and E. E. Payne, named Directors. The proprietor of the store, Leon Haskins, became the Librarian. A membership fee of $2 was collected along with 25¢ monthly dues.

A move, in 1907 to establish a free library with a reading room, was promoted by members of the Greater Medford Club, a sort of Chamber of Commerce. The next year, by resolution of the City Council, "pursuant to the provisions of the statutes of the State of Oregon," a room in the City Hall was designated as a free reading room and library, where anyone could come and go during office hours. Leon Haskins donated the collection of books, that had been kept in the drug store, to the new library.

In 1910, the City Council applied for and received a Carnegie library grant of $20,000. The formula used in asking for this amount of money was based on $2 per person for a population of 10,000. This money would build a library on a site earlier donated for the purpose by Jacksonville's banker, Cornelius C. Beekman and his wife Julia. Beekman was one of the four founders of Medford. The location, on W. Main Street, had earlier been occupied by the town's water tower.

The city needed to also contribute some money to the project so a special election sought an appropriation of 10 percent of the Carnegie grant. The ballot was favorable.

In preparation for the opening of the new library, Miss Elizabeth Robinson was hired by the Library Board as Librarian

at a salary of $80 per month. She was on duty for the grand opening celebration on Thursday, February 8, 1912, when the new library was formally presented to the city. For entertainment, the high school orchestra, which was directed by the school superintendent, Mr. Collins, played during the event. The hours of availability of the library were published:

Open to the Public
Monday through Friday
2:00 p.m. to 5:00 p.m.
7.00 p.m. to 9.00 p.m.
Saturday
9:00 a.m. to 12:00 noon

A letter from the State Librarian made specific suggestions for operations. The local librarian would use three hours daily to work uninterrupted with the door closed. The duties included book selection, purchasing, the intellectual assignment of the Dewey Decimal System numbers to the books and the building of a card catalog. The librarian handled all secretarial record keeping including correspondence. She was to keep the floor swept and the books and shelves dusted. She was to serve the public during the "open" hours. The work week was specified as

43 hours. A post script on the letter mentioned that it was hoped that an assistant would be available soon!

And one was. In January 1913, Miss Mildred Brown was hired at $25.00 per month, then a second assistant, Miss Paxon joined the staff in April 1914.

Ledward reported:

By the end of 1909 the library held 1,744 books, had 1,512 registered patrons with circulation of books reaching 9,000. Fines collected for tardy return of books, $54.38.

By the end of 1910 there were 1,926 books, 1,814 patrons. Circulation not listed. Fines collected, $72.23.

In 1912, the library had a telephone installed and paid a total bill of $19.45 for telephone service for the year.

In 1913 the library held 4,084 books – 1,243 added in the year; 70 periodical titles and circulated 37,829 items averaging 122 items for each day.

In October 1919, Miss Robinson, who by now was receiving $100 each month, retired and was awarded a bonus of $100.

Fringe benefits were allowed starting in 1920 when the Board voted to permit pay for sick days to be earned at the rate of one-half day for each full months service.

Starting in 1920, the Medford library provided a rotating assortment of 50 books among the various small town libraries in the county library system.

In 1923, a newspaper clipping for June 8 declared: "Jackson County is second in the state in library work" and is "again holding second place to Multnomah County." The number of circulations were just under 98,000 from the collection of 13,291 books for 5,700 patrons. In Medford, 67 percent of the people used the library with circulation at 12.1 books per capita.

In 1932, the Board announced that one full month vacation would be allowed after working one year with a provision that no resignations would be accepted until two months after a vacation. But due to the Great Depression, the Board voted a schedule of reduced wages starting August 1.

In December 1933, the librarian reported average daily attendance in the library was 425 patrons with a high circulation on one day reaching 748 items. In addition, the first report of "reference questions" was mentioned with "10 to 20 questions to be answered" in the month.

The beginning of World War-II brought a plea for donations of books to be "send to our men in uniform." Over 700 books were forwarded to the State Library from the Medford area for this purpose then with the startup of Camp White's library, another plea for donations was successful.

In 1942 a salary increase was voted by the Board but the increase would be paid with fine money collected.

It appears that the Carnegie Library's roof had a habit of leaking rather frequently during winter storms and this had been occurring starting with the second year of occupancy. Accordingly, there was a constant drain on the limited funds in an effort to keep water out of the building. The inconvenience of placing buckets and wash tubs on the floor to catch the drips became too much to tolerate thus in 1925, a contract was let for a complete new roof – $281.25 – but two years later, the job had to be repeated. This time the roof lasted until 1935. After dabbling with temporary repairs during the war, a complete reconstruction of the roof was done in 1952 and again in 1962.

Another continuing challenge was trouble with water running "up." When a ship's hull leaks, the skipper turns on pumps. In the Carnegie library, there was such severe seepage in the basement that an ejection pump was installed. But it wouldn't keep things dry so a larger pump replaced the first pump. There were many head-scratchings trying to determine where all the basement water was coming from when someone noted that there was an underground stream flowing under the building!

While the nature of what material the basement floor had been constructed seems elusive, the Board voted to install a "cement floor" and repair the front pillars in 1927.

The library had been heated with a wood-burning furnace and there were complaints about a shrinking in the wood pile (theft!) therefore tall shrubbery was planted to conceal the fire wood from the passersby.

The old incandescent lights what hung from the ceiling were replaced with "modern" fixtures in 1939. But the library's campus was without a flag pole until 1955.

A new wing to be added to the badly over-crowded original building was discussed starting in 1944 with a plan submitted to the voters in a special election on June 12, 1945 (the war was still on but was winding down) for $102,000. This was titled "Library Enlargement and Equipment Bonds Amendment." It passed 582/445. But the haggle over the plans had just begun. By 1949, the City Planning Commission recommended that all bids be rejected and bonds and certified checks be returned to bidders. The delay in taking action was causing strain as the condition of the 1911 building had become acute to the point that the Library Board requested immediate action by the mayor and city council or the members of the Board would resign.

Even with the threat, much time was still required. It was not until 1952 that the building and furnishing were ready for full use with the price tag at $100,678.72 against the bond of $102,000. The balance was consumed in extras.

The library took membership in the Pacific Northwest Library Association (PNLA) in January 1955 and since that time, has participated in service from the bibliographic center and inter-library loan program between all member libraries on request. The service continues to the present time.

The matter of what to do with out-dated books and books worn beyond repair through much usage. Suggestions for burning them to storing them were discussed. The only conclusion reached what that used books could be sold to the public for a nominal amount, the proceeds of the sales going to the city treasury with credit to the library budget. (Annual book sales by the Friends of the Library presently bring in substantial sums.)

Reference services were first announced as available to the public in 1956. An article in the January 11, *Mail Tribune* invited the patrons wishing reference service could call the library between 4 p.m. and 9 p.m. pn Monday, Tuesday or Wednesday. Three months later, the newspaper did a followup story in which the reporter wrote that the reference "service was meeting an increasing demand." By 1965, the Reference Desk was open daily from 9 a.m. to 9 p.m. with an average of 400 questions being handled each month.

In the late 1950's there was a shortage of professional staff and shortage of money but circulation had reached an annual count of 200,000 items.

A change in attitude on the part of librarians nation wide saw the acceptance of "paperback" books as accessioned library items. Medford joined this movement partially because the public demanded it, and partially as the costs of hardcase books was on the increase.

> That the Medford citizens loves their library is evident by the record of library usage. This is largely measured by the records of circulated materials and a count of the number of reference questions handled. If a library has a large patronage, it is because the selection of books and periodicals and provision for other services, like an active Reference Department, is taken very seriously. If a library has what the people seek, then the library will be very busy. Every library in the Jackson County Library Services is busy every open hour.

Over the years there had been a series of librarians, some staying considerable lengths of time, others for shorter periods. Mr. Omar Bacon accepted the appointment as Head Librarian (later changed to "Director") in November 1959. He left in March 1971 followed by Mr. Hardin Smith who retired in February 1987. He was succeeded by Mrs. Ronnie Budge.

There had been a few informal meetings in earlier years with librarians from surrounding towns to brainstorm various methods of improving services. But there was nothing formal until June of 1968, when a serious cooperative effort was made with other libraries throughout Southern Oregon to better serve the people of the local and extended area. The Southern Oregon Library Federation came into being with membership open to any public, school, college, corporate or special libraries in the area.

In 1970, there was a merger of all libraries in Jackson County into the present county-wide system. The headquarters library is in the Medford Branch.

The Jackson County Library Services operates fifteen branches coordinated from the Branches Department in the Medford library. In addition, the Law Library, which serves primarily attorneys, is located in the Justice Building. The Children's Department is not "just kids' books," but has offered "story hour" for the toddlers for a number of years. There are special reading

System-wide old-style catalog cards gave way to computer terminals including in the Children's Department of each branch.

programs for the elementary ages including an extensive summer agenda to keep kids reading. There are now computer terminals replacing the card catalog for the youngsters' use.

In an effort to provide a setting where "teens," especially among those in the younger teen set, would no longer be shunted into the children's department, or become overwhelmed "upstairs" with adults, the specialized Teen Library was opened. It provides a comfortable setting and was accepted immediately by the intended age group.

There is TTY service for the deaf, Outreach to Senior Citizens and the Homebound, and an Outreach Program to Day Care providers.

The traditional style card catalog, where there were thousands of 3 x 5-inch cards representing every book in the library, gave way to a computer catalog which any patron of the library can use with minimal instruction. In addition, persons with home computers can access the "catalog" from their homes and businesses and reserve books to be later checked out.

Years ago, the circulation department did away with writing

In Medford Main Branch, terminals for the computer catalog of 424,380 books and audio-visual items are, in the adult department, on high tables for stand-up use. Shelves in background hold some of the Reference Department's books. Medford Reference personnel answered 62,513 questions between July 1 1995 and June 30, 1996.

borrowers names and "due dates" in record books and turned to book charge-out machines. In Medford, this was an efficient system for its time (and is still in use in thousands of smaller libraries nationwide). The county-wide system with many thousands of books, video tapes, cassette tapes, periodicals, maps and other circulatable material, converted to BAR-CODE and a theft detection system to better keep track of its materials. The BAR-CODE speeds the check-out process as well as the check-in system for clearing patron records and placing loaned items back on shelves.

The Medford Reference Center, with Ann Billeter, Ph.D. as head of Adult Reader Services, has a staff of 10 professional librarians, 9 paraprofessionals plus a specialist volunteer. There is also a Business Reference Librarian who specializes in business and computer access matters for the business community. A special clerk coordinates a large inter-library loan service. The library is severely over-crowded with its tremendous book collection, the number of librarians required to service it all and

All branches of the Jackson County Library Services use a computer-managed circulation system. Picture shows the Medford checkout desk. (LOWER) Each patron holds a library card on the reverse of which is a BAR-CODE for that patron.

the number of daily patrons who throng the premises. It is obvious that a new building is a high-demand item.

Compare the present operations and staff to the opening days of the library in Haskins' Drug Store and a little later when Miss Robinson did everything in the new (present) building including the sweeping of the floor. ◇

Editor's note: The area code shown on library card, "503," was changed by the telephone company to "541" on July 1, 1996.

First Plane Lands in Medford

In 1909, this aeroplane made of cloth covered bamboo, landed in a field near Medford to participate in an air show. However, Medford's altitude was too high for the plane to take off so admission charge to onlookers had to be refunded. When the plane was towed to lower ground, the pilot, Mr. Ely, took off and left town. But the next summer he came back and successfully provided his flying exhibition. This is thought to be the first plane to land in Medford.

—6—

Medford Airport Has Many Notable "Firsts"

In 1919, Seeley Hall and Floyd Hart, just back from the First World War and service in the Signal Corps Air Service, bought a used Curtis Jenny airplane. This was the first airplane owned in Medford. The men had a good business flying people over the valley on sightseeing tours from landing fields on ranches between Medford and Jacksonville. They formed Medford Aircraft Corporation in 1920.

Because the Forest Service needed a field from which to operate patrols on the lookout for forest fires, Medford and Jackson County bought some land between the fair grounds and Bear Creek and named it for a war hero, Newell Barber. This was in 1922. Newell Barber Field became the first field in Oregon to be purchased specifically for use as an airport. Its major use then was as a home for the U. S. Forest Service Air Patrol.

Medford's airport got off to a blasting start as gravel, a few pieces at a time from its runway, 1,500 feet long and 25 feet wide, was whipped into a frenzy by the prop wash of the airplanes which threw rocks at anyone who was standing in the wrong place.

The Forest Service chose Medford because there had been a series of very damaging forest fires in the area. At that time, the fairgrounds-airport was on the far south edge of town, near today's south freeway interchange, about where the baseball field is presently located.

To speed delivery of letter mail, the Post Office Department opened an Air Mail service in May 1918 between Washington, Philadelphia and New York City. As time went on and this experimental service proved itself, other routes were assigned. One of these routes called for service between Los Angeles and Se-

(ABOVE) **Ernie Scott (right), with his 1924 Harley Davidson motorcycle, has just delivered mail to the Medford airport from the town's post office. In the picture are (left to right) Bill Rosenbaum, chief mechanic for Pacific Air Transport, Pat Patterson, pilot, William Warner, Medford postmaster and Roland G. Beach, Assistant postmaster.** (LOWER) **Ryan M-1 all-metal monoplane flew the first air mail in Oregon from Medford on September 15, 1926.**

Seely Hall and Verne C. Gorst,
founded Pacific Air Transport.
Hall became the first Superintendent (Director) of the Medford
airport.

Vern Gorst became
known as the "Father
of the Air Mail Service
on the Pacific Coast."
Gorst was respon-
sible for originating
air mail service on
the Pacific Coast. The
first flight was from
Medford.

attle. It was necessary to have a mid-point along the way and the Department decided this would be in Southern Oregon.

Official fingers were pointing in Ashland's direction for a landing field but Seely Hall announced that Ashland could never be satisfactory because of the closeness of the Siskiyou Mountains. This was long before radio guidance systems. The early airplanes usually had only altimeter, compass, and a stop-watch for instruments. Getting in and out of Ashland, he maintained, would be tricky.

Verne C. Gorst, an entrepreneur who lived in Medford and was involved in a variety of enterprises, was able to obtain a contract for hauling mail by air from Los Angeles to Seattle. He learned that Ashland's name had come up only because the Post Office Department knew it had a railroad terminal.

West Coast Air Mail Joins Seattle, Medford, San Francisco and Los Angeles

| SEATTLE | MEDFORD | SAN FRANCISCO | LOS ANGELES |

●-------------------------◆----------------------------●---------------●

Gorst convinced the Department to change the designated mid-point in the long flight to Medford. He pointed out that Medford already had an operating field and was ready to go.

Gorst and Hall, and some others, founded the Pacific Air Transport, Inc. then Paul McKee, President of the California-Oregon Power Company, helped Hall in locating stockholders at $100 per share. Without hesitation, some stock was sold to business men, a few becoming major investors.

Medford awarded a lease on the airport to Pacific Air Transport, Inc. in September 1926. The lease was for four years for which the young air carrier paid a fee of $1. Pacific Air Transport built a hanger and office building. Next, Gorst and Seely they set off for San Diego to buy the best airplanes available that would safely carry mail.

They bought Ryan M-1 all-metal monoplanes similar to that which Charles Lindbergh used on his epic flight across the Atlantic Ocean. With the Wright Whirlwind 200 horse power engine, a hop between Medford and San Francisco was just 3½ hours. *

The first flight of the new Air Mail service, operated by Pacific Air Transport, took off from Medford on Wednesday, September 15, 1926. Pat Patterson was the pilot. A full page advertisement in the Medford *Mail Tribune* announced the service and hawked that a letter would get to Portland in 2½ hours; a letter for New York would be there in 36 hours.

This was the first Air Mail service in Oregon and it was started in Medford! (Air Mail for Portland landed at Pangborn Field in Vancouver.)

> **It was not long before Vern Gorst became known as the "Father of the Air Mail Service on the Pacific Coast"**

Three years later, Pacific Air Transport merged with two other regional lines, Boeing Air Transport and Varney Airlines. This business adjustment formed United Air Lines. This was in September of 1929 and United Air Lines has been serving the Medford area's people ever since.

Seely Hall, Superintendent for Pacific Air Transport, became the first Director of the Medford Airport, until 1931.

Air travel by the public was on the verge of taking off. The limited facilities at the fair grounds field was already overtaxed so a committee of the Medford Chamber of Commerce was appointed in 1928 to look for a better site. Consultations were held with the U. S. Department of Commerce – Aviation Department, with the Army, and with representatives of interested air carriers, then operating in the area, all being asked for opinions.

The Department of Commerce had definite ideas about what would constitute a Class-A Field. The field (the early term for "airport"), to be certified as an Intermediate Field, to service aircraft and passenger between two main terminals – as between

---

*After May of 1927, Boeing Model 40 bi-planes became available. This plane carried the pilot, 2 passengers and 1,200 pounds of mail. Between 1929 and 1932, new model Boeing 40B-4 bi-planes carried 4 passengers, the pilot and 500 pounds of mail. These airplanes had a range of 535 miles in still air with its 525 hp Pratt & Whitney Hornet engine. The plane cost $24,500. The Boeings became a common sight at the Medford airport. In recent years, the wreckage of a Boeing 40, which crashed about 1927, was discovered in the mountains near Medford. The remains have been salvaged for eventual rebuilding as a non-flying exhibit for an air museum.

aircraft and passenger between two main terminals – as between Portland and San Francisco – would require, in addition to an Administration Building, a hangar, restaurant, gasoline and oil availability. The landing strip would have to be lighted for night flights. Of course, the airport would have a rotating beacon, and there needed to be a weather office. The runway was required to be at least one mile long in the middle of a half-mile wide parcel. The Chamber, in the role of chairman of the inquiry, finally announced that by unanimous agreement, a 238 acre site, about three miles north of Medford near Biddle Road, was the choice. The land was purchased for $28,000 and construction started. The work, with a bill of $120,000, was completed in October 1929. The project was covered by a bond issue with near unanimous approval of the people of Medford.

The new Medford Municipal Airport had, as its night time signature, a 2,550,000 candlepower beacon. Everything was state-of-the-art including a weather bureau and radio station.

There was a "Hotel DeGink," the slang name for the overnight rooms provided for enroute pilots. Standard Oil Company and five more fuel companies had pumps. The Medford airport was classed as "big time." The open house and dedication of the new field on August 4, 1930, was highlighted with a demonstration by Tex Rankin who was the guest of honor. Rankin was a world-famous stunt flyer and aerobatic expert.

A great innovation in the design of airplanes for passenger service was the short era of tri-motor, all-metal transports. In the U.S. both Ford Motor Company and Boeing Airplane Company built "tin goose" tri-motors. The first of these to land in Medford, on a daily basis, on a new run between Oakland and Seattle, was on November 1, 1930. Records do not reveal if it was a Ford or Boeing.

Hall stayed as Medford Superintendent of PAT for four years then went to Los Angeles. With the merger, he became General Manager for Ground Services with United. He always had a soft spot in his heart for the Medford airport and was the invited guest for the 20th anniversary of the Airport in 1949.

Over the years, the airport added more space until it presently occupies 925 acres. A 100-foot wide cross-runway 2,805 feet

(TOP) Pacific Air Transport terminal at Medford with Boeing Model 40 mail plane on right. (LOWER) Every time the Medford airport held an air show, the people turned out. This is still true to the present time. Large airplane in center is a tri-motor.

Administration building and hangar was
designed by architect Frank C. Clark.

Military Considerations

In the 1930's, the 60th Pursuit Squadron from Hamilton Field, north of San Francisco, used the Medford airport for summer training.

During World War-II, the War Department replaced civilian management of many municipal airports throughout the United States. In Medford, Air Force personnel, stationed at the airport, put up their own small barracks and administrative office. In addition, the CAA (Civil Aeronautics Authority – forerunner to the FAA) supplied air traffic controllers to operate the tower under strict war-time regulations.

United Airlines Douglas DC-3 aircraft, the major passenger plane of the time, came and departed on regular schedules but with special "Priorities" required for a person to get a ticket. Airlines profited as the planes –21 seats – were always full.

Private passengers were at great risk of being "bumped" out of their seat without notice if a person, usually Air Force pilots or military officers on travel orders, needed the seat. Getting "bumped" became an unfortunate but common, war-time hazard at many airports. Medford was an airport where a high-risk of losing a seat existed due to nearby Camp White. If a non-priority through passenger (Portland - San Francisco) was enjoying his flight and an officer from the camp appeared with travel orders, the civilian could be deplaned. He could be stuck in Medford for days waiting for an open seat but most people, when "bumped," continued by train or Greyhound bus.

(TOP) **Passenger terminal at Rogue Valley International Medford Airport** (CENTER AND LOWER) **United Airlines celebrated 70 years of service in Medford in 1996.**
(LOWER) **Passengers exit** COMMUTE-A-WALK **and head for aircraft.**

long was constructed. As aircraft with higher power and greater carrying capacity were built, the airport continued to expand to handle the traffic. The landing strip was extended to 6,700 feet.

The first full cargo transcontinental shipment of fresh fruit, flowers and fish ever flown, left Medford for LaGuardia Field in New York City on a United Airlines DC-3 cargoliner on August 22, 1944. This was a demonstration flight to show the post-war practicability of shipping fresh perishables coast-to-coast by air.

When the war was over, United Airlines quickly found competition vying for its Medford passengers. Southwest Airways, a predecessor to Hughes Air West, started flights in December 1946. Then in almost regular order others flew in then flew out.

Carrier	Date Started	Terminated
Pacific Air Transport	Sep. 1926	Sep. 1929 (became part of UAL)
United Air Lines	**Sep. 1929**	**Operating**
Southwest Airways	Dec. 1946	Predecessor to Hughes Air West
West Coast Airlines	Jul. 1947	Predecessor to Hughes Air West
Hughes Air West	Aug. 1968	Mar. 1979
Pacific Northern	Oct. 1973	Nov. 1973
Air Oregon	Oct. 1978	May 1982
Far West Airlines	Oct. 1979	May 1980
Century Airlines	Nov. 1980	Mar. 1981
Pacific Express	Jan. 1982	Feb. 1984
Horizon Air (Div. Of Alaska Airlines)	**Mar. 1982**	**Operating**
Cascade Airways	Nov. 1984	Sep. 1985
Pacific South West	Dec. 1985	Dec. 1987
Continental Airlines	Apr. 1987	May 1988
United Express	**Sep. 1987**	**Operating**
U S Air	Jan. 1988	Sep. 1990
Advantage Airlines	May 1992	Jul. 1992
Reno Air	Oct. 1994	Feb. 1995
FunJet Express	Feb. 1995	Nov. 1955
Sierra Expressway	Aug. 1995	Feb. 1996

The Medford airport has traditionally experienced "difficult days" in winter months caused by persistent, heavy, fog. In 1948, the ILS (Instrument Landing System) was installed but in zero-visibility fog, the airport was often closed sometimes for days at a time.

In January of 1971, the airport was transferred from city to county ownership. By May of 1973, working with the Medford Fire Department, the Medford-Jackson County Airport, as it was then known, provided 24-hour crash-rescue protection. The new Fire Station, with dormitories for firemen was occupied in 1985.

A series of federal grants provided for runway and taxiway reconditioning, a helipad and an access control. In late 1993, the director serving the airport the longest, Gunther "Gunnar" E. Katzmar (1979-1993) retired after completing the new expanded terminal and after securing over $13 million in federal grants for construction and improvements. Bern E. Case* came aboard as Airport Director in January 1994.

* Case, a friendly but keen businessman, made headlines when a commuter air-line gave only a few *minutes* notice that it was leaving, with passengers, on its last flight. Case, with his fingers on the pulse of airport operations, knew that the carrier was behind several thousands of dollars in fee payments. He reason-ed, quickly, if that airplane left the ground it seemed likely all the over-due money would be lost. He promptly seized the aircraft by ordering the fire trucks to park in front and in back of it. This no-nonsense handling of the matter won raves of approval from the public. It was a number of days before the money, $16,000, showed up. When it did, Bern Case removed the fire trucks and the airplane was free to depart.

Ford-built Tri-Motor
passenger planes
stopped in Medford.

<u>Medford, First in Fog Dispersal</u>

Bombing With Dry Ice Turns Fog Into Mild Snow Storm

In 1963, United Airlines chose Medford's airport for fog-dispersal experiments. These experiments, for seeding super-cooled fog, were very extensive but are simply explained.

George Milligan, a pilot and FAA Air Traffic Controller assigned to the Medford tower, was hired for the experiments.

With a hole cut in the bottom of a small airplane, a person pushed crushed dry ice through the hole into the fog. The equipment for the operation was a dishpan with a hole to match the opening cut in the airplane floor, a screened length of 4-inch irrigation pipe, and a small shovel.

Dry ice was shoveled into the pan then the pieces of dry ice, which have a tendency to stick together, are separated by an assistant and shoved through the hole. The dry ice converts the super-cooled fog (small water droplets) into ice crystals. These miniature crystals attract other crystals within seconds, becoming large enough to fall to the ground as a fine snow storm. The result is a channel cut through the fog over a runway allowing aircraft to land or take off.

Milligan had a dedicated interest in the experiments as he was the founder of Mercy Flights, the nations first certified Air Ambulance. His air ambulance needed to fly on short notice therefore a method of fog dispersal had to be found.

coping covered walkway. Medford's COMMUTE-A-WALK is the first one installed on the Pacific Coast of only three in the nation at this writing. The unit can be extended from the terminal door to steps leading up to an airplane.

Visiting war-bird, a World War-II Boeing B-17 bomber at Medford airport in spring 1996. Several times a year organizations that own this and other propeller-driven aircraft, particularly former military bombers and fighter planes, attract crowds who are very willing to pay a fee to climb aboard the planes, sit in the pilot's seat, crawl into the tail-gunners position and "hanger-fly" (talk) with the crew.

Because the role of the airport was changing, a public contest was held for a new name. In January 1995, the Foreign-Trade Zones Board of the United States Department of Commerce announced that Jackson County had been awarded the newest foreign-trade zone in the country. The Medford site is 95 acres on the east side of the airport within the airport security fence. The U. S. Customs and Immigration Service has a presence as the airport is now an International Port of Entry. As a result of the contest the wining name was

ROGUE VALLEY INTERNATIONAL-MEDFORD AIRPORT

Although on a need-it-now list with the FAA for many years, a new radar system went into service on April 20, 1995. The purpose is to provide precise locations for aircraft in the vicinity and to reduce risk of collisions.

The Medford airport is a place of constant activity and is wholly self-supporting with no local or state taxes used. ⬦

7

Fighting Forest Fires with Airplanes

Load 'em up, fly to target, "bombs away," head for home. Pickup another load, take off, "bombs away," head for home. Do it again and again.

But these bombers are not carrying high-explosive blockbusters but on each trip, each bomber delivers between 800 and 3,500 gallons of fire retardant on a forest fire.

The Medford airport has been home to the Forest Service Air Patrols since its earliest days and now hosts the Medford Fire Center. This is an operations office for directing the fighting against forest fires.

Immediately after World War-II, B-24 and B-17 four-engine heavy bombers, and lighter craft as B-25 and B-26 twin engine bombers, were being converted by adding large belly tanks to fuselages. It was not uncommon to see former Navy Catalina flying boat patrol bombers on the Medford strip in the new role of fire fighter. As jet aircraft forced propeller-driven passenger planes out of the skies, DC-4, DC-6, and DC-7 and other types were converted to fire fighters. The former deluxe United Air Lines *City of Los Angeles* DC-7 now resembles a pregnant guppy with its belly tank, often operated from Medford.

Medford is in a valley surrounded by dense forests. When summer thunderstorms strike, there are often more than a dozen independent fires started as the result of a single storm. Based on various conditions, especially how dry are the forests, fire can spread quickly requiring maximum effort – and lots of money – to contain them then put them out.

In 1987, the Silver Complex Fire in Southern Oregon burned 96,240 acres. While the smoke nearly blotted out the sun, the ash was so thick it rained on Medford streets like snowflakes.

These privately owned aircraft are chartered by the Forest Service with planes sent to appropriately equipped airports clo-

"Bombing" forest fires with liquid fire retardant or with heavy doses of water has been a long standing method of fighting forest fires. The Medford Fire Center at the Medford airport can sometimes seem to be in a state of frenzy with the rapid loading of as much as 3,500 gallons of retardant then the dispatch of the "bombers" to a fire. Many former World War-II bombing planes as the B-17 (ABOVE) have been adapted for this service. One of the best aircraft for this work are former DC-7 deluxe passenger planes (LOWER) to which 3,000 gallon tanks have been added.

(ABOVE) **DC-7 former deluxe passenger plane, converted to fire fighter, rests at Medford Fire Center. In rear is C-46 former Air Force transport. Plane is owned by Erickson Air-Crane, is used for heavy cargo.** (LOWER) **Storage tanks at Medford Fire Center.**

sest to the fires. Flying a fire fighting bomber is an exciting, serious, dangerous business and none of the pilots take their work lightly. Doing dive bombing with former passenger planes is by-the-numbers flying for the minimum altitude at which it is best to dump is just 75 feet off the ground.

At an airport's fire fighting base are special tanks of liquid mix of concentrated ammonium sulphate fertilizer and water – the retardant. The Medford Fire Center can create up to 125,000 gallons of retardant at a time and can fill the belly tanks of airplanes within minutes. In a very troubled summer, a single fire base might deliver as much as 1,000,000 gallons of retardant on fires in a single month. On one 24-hour day at the Medford base, there were 38 trips that dropped 114,000 gallons.

With the modern radar equipment at the airport and alert control tower operators, the three elements of flying, commercial passenger airplanes, forest service fire bombers, and general aviation share the space with minimum risk ⬦

8

Gas-Jockey Becomes Airport Director

Medford Airport's "Boy Manager" (1931-1942) Tom A. Culbertson, Jr., became interested in flying by associating with early Pacific Air Transport pilots at Newell Barber Field. He was an 11 year old Medford school kid engrossed with flying.

When he was 19 (1928), Charles Lindbergh, who had solo-flown the Atlantic Ocean just a year earlier, made an unpublicized visit to Medford. Culbertson's enthusiasm for flying was cemented into place for life when he met "Lindy" and was permitted to sit in his airplane although the plane was similar to but not the famous Ryan "Spirit of St. Louis."

Culbertson graduated from high school in Medford, tried college but decided he's rather fly, got his pilot's license, was an advocate for a new flying field, operated a flying service and by age 22, was appointed manager of the Medford airport. In the 1930's, he was a member of the State Board of Aeronautics.

In 1929, he took flying lessons from Harry Crandall, one of the air mail pilots. Culbertson received a pilot's license then in 1931, he was awarded a limited commercial license.

Seely Hall, the Superintendent at the airport, hired him to gas the airplanes at 2¢ a gallon, wash them and keep the constant dust swept out of the hangar that blew in from the gravel runway. The gas-jockey job paid well as Medford was the only stop for hungry airplanes going both north and south.

Culbertson's first airplane was an OX5 Travelair bi-plane be and Bill Rosenbaum Sr., a PAT mechanic, bought in 1930. Culbertson went into the Air Force in 1942 eventually rising to the rank of Colonel. He spent 56 years in and around the Medford airport watching it grow from a dusty, rock-throwing gravel runway to the present modern jet-age facility. ◇

—From microfilm of *Mail Tribune*

—9—
Lone Eagle" Charles Lindbergh, at Medford Airport

After Lindbergh's epic trans-Atlantic flight, he toured the U.S. in his "Spirit of St. Louis" Ryan monoplane. Although not generally publicized, due to Lindbergh's utter dislike of reporters, he avoided telling the press where he was going.

On Friday, September 16, 1927, he over-flew Medford in his ocean-hopping Ryan on his flight from Portland to San Francisco (7 hrs and 5 min.).

It is important to note that the Ryan Monoplane Lindbergh flew and landed in Medford in 1928 is not identified as to its model, but his "Spirit of St. Louis" by that time had been given to the Smithsonian Institution where it is presently exhibited. His last flight in the New York-to-Paris Ryan was on April 30, 1928 from St. Louis to Bolling Field, Washington, D.C. where the Smithsonian accepted it.

The "Spirit of St. Louis," a Ryan all-metal monoplane flown by Charles A. Lindbergh non-stop from New York to Paris on May 20-21, 1927. About four months later, he flew this airplane over Medford but he did not drop in.

(The "Spirit of St. Louis" was originally an M-1 design but Ryan built Lindbergh's airplane for the flight to Paris to custom specifications and called it an "M-2." They did the work in about 60 days for $6,000 (less engine and instruments). It carried 362 gallons of gasoline and could fly about 4,000 miles non-stop.)

Lindbergh's Second Medford Visit

Lindbergh was again on the ground in Medford on Tuesday, July 4, 1939. This time he was flying a new Curtis P-36 Army Air Corps pursuit-interceptor airplane. Just before leaving for Medford, the plane went through its 40-hour check at Hamilton Field north of San Francisco. From his diary:

It was overcast at the Oregon [/California] border and I followed the valleys with their streams and roads. Passed through several local storms and landed at Medford at 16:45 P.T [Pacific time]. Medford is one of the Army fuel stations, with Army personnel to take care of fueling. While I was there, the field manager – it is a small place – asked me to come sometime and go fishing. He reminded me of the time I had stopped in Medford in 1928 with my Ryan monoplane in which I brought Tom Eastland [a California businessman who was influential in organizing Transcontinental Air Transport], and one or two of his friends for a short vacation. We went to a cabin in high timber, on the side of a trout stream.

Took off from Medford at 17.11 P.T. The rest of my flight [to Seattle] was under overcast skies. I followed valleys and detoured the cloud-covered mountains, trying to keep high enough above the trees to be able to jump in case my motor stopped. This plane [with 1,200 hp engine] lands too fast to permit getting down safely in anything but a fairly level field. I had decided

LINDBERGH HERE FOR BRIEF VISIT ENROUTE NORTH

Lone Eagle Checks Weather Data and Refuels

—Microfilm, Medford *Mail Tribune*

Charles Augustus Lindbergh
Colonel, USAF-Res. (1902-1974)
Seated in P-36 fighter plane.
In World War-II in the Pacific, he was a technical
representative to the U. S. Air Force, flew 50 combat
missions against the Japanese and shot down several.

99

that if there were not a good-sized clearing or farm field within gliding range, I would cut the switch, pull the plane up into a stall, and jump. There would be no use riding it down into those great tree tops of the northwest.

Lindbergh's non-stop flight from Medford to Seattle in the fighter plane took only 1 hour 55 minutes.

His visit at Medford's airport was strictly for gasoline as he was on the ground only 26 minutes! He mentions the "field manager" who was Tom Culbertson. Lindbergh said of Medford "it is a small place" and plausibly the only person around, between airline passenger schedules, was the "manager" – Culbertson. Although Culbertson mentions Lindbergh's 1928 visit in a *Mail Tribune* article of his recollections published on June 6, 1985, there is no mention of Lindbergh's 1939 visit when Lindy flew in for gas in an Army fighter plane.

Charles A. Lindbergh, a Colonel in the U. S. Air Corps Reserve, stopping by in a fighter plane, was a newsworthy event but the Medford *Mail Tribune* didn't know about it until prompted by a wire service story, datelined Seattle, that arrived the next day. The paper printed the piece on July 5th under headline "Lindbergh Here For Brief Visit."

Col. Charles A. Lindbergh, in a jovial mood but adhering to his policy of not discussing his plans for newspapers publication, spent half an hour yesterday at Medford municipal airport while enroute from Sunnyvale, Cal. to Boeing Field, Seattle, Wash.

The story said that there was no advance notice given to Seattle newspapers that the famous pilot was coming. But his mission was revealed after Lindbergh had left Seattle. He met with Howard Hughes, who arrived using an alias on a commercial flight, and with the Boeing president and a Boeing test pilot, and Civil Aeronautics Authority men on official business.

The *Mail Tribune* contributed to the story by interviewing Airport Director Tom Culbertson who said: "The colonel appeared almost as young and boyish as he did on his previous call here about 10 years ago."

Culbertson, who met the famed aviator on his previous visit and conversed with him yesterday, said "the colonel recalled his Medford stop of a decade ago with a feeling of pleasure." ◇

National Weather Service Gets
Early Start Here

When the Medford airport opened in 1926, the National
Weather Service was there. In 1996 it's still there only better
and bigger.

Before the advent of the airport, the weather was monitored,
starting on March 11, 1911 by the county extension agents in
town. But about all they recorded were temperatures, humidity
and rain. While these remain components of weather observation and forecasting, these factors alone are inadequate for pilots
who also need to know, among other things, the altitudes at
which various air currents are moving, in which directions and
at what speeds?

In 1917, the first fruit frost forecasts began in Medford and
was operated from the county agent's office in town. The forecast was given to the telephone operator and orchardists would
call the operator for the information.

Delbert M. Little, Jr. arrived to establish and take charge of
the Weather Bureau Airways Station in Medford on December
11, 1926. By December 15, instrumentation such as hydrogen
tanks, balloons, scales, plotting boards, forms and supplies arrived allowing the office to officially open on December 22,
1926. The first official observation was taken at 7:20 a.m. The
forecast was made available to Pacific Air Transport Service
office at Pangborn Field at Vancouver, Washington. There a
chart of the entire Pacific Coast was hand drawn thus showing a
picture of what the firm's pilots would encounter along the way.
In 1929, teletype circuits on leased telephone lines patched the
Medford and Portland weather offices together.

Doppler RADAR meets the sky above highest peak on Mt. Ashland. To left (out of view) is transmitter for KTVL-TV, Medford, with highest TV tower, 7.533 ft. elev., in Oregon

During World War II, because of a threat of landings on the Oregon beaches by a Japanese invasion force, there were no broadcasts of weather forecasts and forecasts no longer appeared in the daily newspapers. But the meteorological station at the Medford airport was constantly busy with visits by pilots stopping to see weather charts.

The first RADAR on top of Mt. Ashland went to work in June 1971. In August 1979, the NOAA Weather Radio became a part of the National Weather Service in Medford.

Now, radiosonde balloons launched at the Medford airport record readings of wind direction and velocity, temperature and humidity at various levels as the balloons rise. Readings stop when the balloon breaks usually between 70,000 and 110,000 feet altitude. This information, coupled with the RADAR findings and ground observations, are used to prepare forecasts. The Automated Surface Observing System (ASOS) is presently being installed nationwide and will serve as the nation's primary surface weather observing network. ASOS updates observations non-stop, every minute, 24 hours a day, every day of the year.

A major concern of the aviation people is safety, and weather conditions often threaten safety. For aircraft, a primary concern are conditions on the ground when an airplane is about to

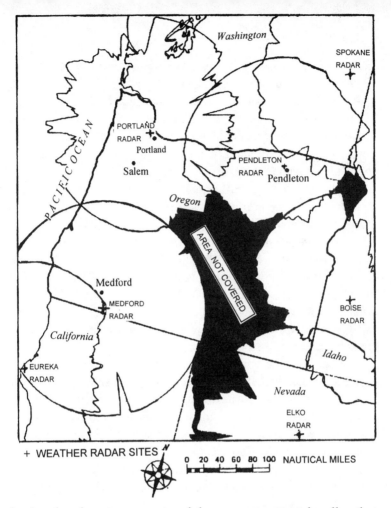

0 20 40 60 80 100 NAUTICAL MILES

land – the airport runway touchdown zones. ASOS handles that with great efficiency.

But the weather service is involved in far more than watching the skies for the benefit of airplane pilots. Some of the daily users are local radio and television reporters. They obtain their reports from the National Weather Service Office of the National Oceanic & Atmospheric Administration at the Medford airport. The office has specially trained forecasters such as those who do spring time fruit frost forecasts for orchardists and others who study the conditions that may lead to summer thunderstorms and forest fires.

In 1995, a modernization of the "weather office" included a

DOPPLER RADAR system. This was installed in place of the old RADAR dome on the very top of Mt. Ashland – 7,533 ft elevation – about 30 air miles to the south. Other nearby NOAA National Weather Services RADAR and forecasting sites are in Eureka, California, Medford, Pendleton, Portland in Oregon and in Boise, Idaho. On the map, it is noted that there are overlaps in the range of each RADAR site.

Older RADAR systems could locate storms but the new systems see *inside* storms and detect wind-driven precipitation that is being carried toward or away from the RADAR.

The DOPPLER drives a super-computer and is sensitive to the point where it will record a single rain drop, speck of dust, an insect – and record the altitude, the wind direction and wind speed of the object. This will improve forecasting and warning capabilities even of small-scale, short-lived and threatening weather events which will allow for early protective measures to be in place before a storm strikes.

Upper-air observations are the basic ingredients of future weather forecasting. It is from the National Weather Service offices at the Medford Airport that forecasts up to ten days in advance are prepared, picked up by broadcasters and transmitted locally as well as to remote areas because of the broadcasters' translators. The Medford weather office has specific interest in Coos, Curry, Douglas, Josephine, Jackson, Lake counties in Oregon and in Siskiyou and Modoc counties of California.◇

—11—

Mercy Flights, Nation's First Air Ambulance

Mercy Flights, Inc. a non-profit Air Ambulance operation, was started by George Milligan in 1949 as an emergency measure primarily to fly polio patients to hospitals in Portland.

From Medford to Portland was about twelve hours by way of the serpentine highway and that was too long for transporting seriously ill patients to the big Portland hospitals. In an airplane, the distance would be covered in less than two hours.

Dozens of airports have charter flying services and patients had traditionally been carried by these, but these airplanes could not carry a stretcher-case.

He recalled when Mercy Flights was started:

There were two essentially county-type hospitals in Medford. Mercy Flights became a service area with those hospitals. Originally we started to carry people out but then we began carrying more people in from the coast and Eastern Oregon. Mostly we carried people to Portland, Eugene, Seattle and San Francisco. The reason we started was because of polio. Polio was a very scary thing. All the polio victims had to go either to Eugene or to Portland and they went by ground.

Clarence Winetrout, who had the Ford agency, came down with polio. Eventually, they had to take him by ground ambulance to Portland and it took twelve hours. They had to stop at several places – Grants Pass, Roseburg, and

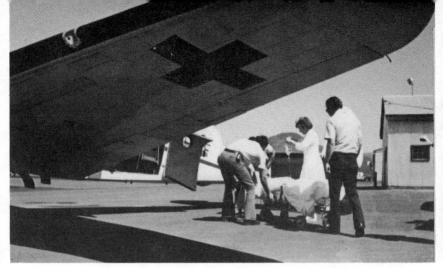

(TOP) **Margie Webber, RN, Flight Nurse, supports IV-feed for emergency air-lift of patient.** (LOWER) **The Mercy Flights Beechcraft D-18 (C-45) transported 1,150 stretcher cases in its 21-years of service with Mercy Flights.**

so on – and give a little care at the hospitals. He died three or four days later as a result of shock.

It would have taken an hour-and-a-half in an airplane. I watched it as I was working in the airport's control tower. We'd get these calls…. 'Where can be get an airplane that we can get a stretcher in"? There just weren't any airplanes big enough for a stretcher. They would have to put [patients] in an airplane and sit them up. I became aware that we had this need and finally reached the place that I figured I'd better do something about it.

After talks with the *Mail Tribune's* editor, Eric Allen, a Board of Directors was "drafted" from the citizens. These were locally well-known people and included the person in charge of

the local polio chapter, a nurse, some doctors, a dentist – twelve in all. Through Allen's editorials in the newspaper, a drive was promoted for nickels and dimes from the citizens, including school kids. Six months later, with $3,400 donated, Mercy Flights bought a war-surplus Cessna "Bob Cat" twin engine airplane. This fabric-covered pilot trainer and light utility aircraft, called a UC-78/AT-17, had its already sparse interior overhauled to accommodate a stretcher, which fit with ease, and room for a nurse-attendant.

Mercy Flights was incorporated as a non-profit organization. The pilots, and the nurses, all volunteered their time and received reimbursement only for out-of-pocket expenses. Milligan was the first pilot. As other flyers became available and as George was the decision-maker, he was appointed by the Board of Directors to hold the title "Chief Pilot."

In 1950, the first full year of operations, Mercy Flights had flown thirteen critically ill patients. Only half of them had any money to pay. Milligan pondered for a way to get money from the public but to give something in return. It was decided to sell Pre-Paid Emergency Air Ambulance Services against the time when people might need it. Milligan recalled:

By April 1951, we were about $800 in debt and I decided to try selling $2 a year family subscriptions. There was a local auctioneer by name of Colonel Burns. He could sell anything. He just started going up and down the street buttonholing people. He did that for a couple of weeks and personally sold $4,000 worth of subscriptions at $2 each.

The plan was simple. If the subscriber's physician certified there was an emergency that could not be handled with a land ambulance, the flight for that patient would be free to a hospital from anywhere within the service area. The service area to hold a subscription was about 150 air miles in a circle from Medford but service was available up to 400 miles. Or, if people were away from home and the emergency arose, Mercy Flights would go get them and fly them back to Medford. Over time, the service area was expanded.

Mercy Flights' air ambulance planes are permanently equipped with oxygen and various medical gear and every patient is attended by an on-board nurse.

The Mercy Flights helicopter can set down in places where winged-aircraft cannot land and on arrival in Medford, can de-plane stretcher patients at either Rogue Valley Medical Center or at Providence Medford Medical Center as each has helicopter pads.

The Cessna airplane gave way to a war-surplus twin engine Beechcraft C-45 transport. It had been used to haul light freight and to train pilots and navigators. In 1959, this plane, nicknamed "Iron Annie," took on white paint with huge red crosses on her rudders and wings to become the first "pure" Air Ambulance in the United States, and it was based in Medford. Although totally air-worthy, the C-45 was pretty cold to fly in, especially on winter flights, as the airplane leaked air. There was no heater.

When VHF Direction Finders became available for civil aircraft, Mercy Flight's Beechcraft D-18 (Army C-45) Air Ambulance was the first aircraft in Southern Oregon to get one.

At airports, either when arriving or ready for take off, the Air Ambulance has priority runway rights over all other aircraft except the President's Plane, Airforce-1. The C-45 served until it was retired in July 1980. At last report, it is on exhibit at an air museum at Boeing Field in Seattle.

The pre-paid plan has been in effect ever since but now, over forty years later, the price is a little higher but the range of air-availability has been increased. Presently, Mercy Flights serves all areas west of the Rocky Mountains, and with its recently acquired land ambulance service in the Rogue Valley, has over 35,000 subscribers.

As time rolled on, Mercy Flights acquired more modern and sophisticated aircraft, including a helicopter, and can operate several at the same time. Over the years, more than twenty airplanes have been used. Its service is unique. To June 7, 1996, Mercy Flights has air-lifted 10,812 stretcher patients. It all started at the Medford airport and continues to this time. ◇

Mercy Flights, so far as is known, is the only organization of its kind in the world. Its support comes from subscribers, thousands of them, and from donations and bequests and by fees charges to non-subscribers.

(TOP) **Pear orchard. Thousands of smudge pots** (INSET) **placed among thousands of fruit trees protect buds from freezing temperatures on early spring mornings. Bins, filled by pickers, are trucked to processing plants in Medford.**

12

Fresh Pears From Medford

In Medford's earlier years, when the fresh fruit business was thriving, many dozens of carefully iced fruit express railway cars pulled out every night for national markets. Not only was the fruit business making big money for the orchardists and packers, it provided full-time work in a peripheral industry – timber. Not a single pear could be shipped without a box to put it in. These were the days when fruit boxes were all made of wood. Some mills made nothing but fruit boxes.

The orchard business is changing. While the buildings that once housed "cannery row," in south Medford are still standing, the whole-fruit canning operations have moved elsewhere. But there is a specialty business, Sabroso Company, that only cans pear nectar, but its "cans" are a little too large for a kitchen pantry – 55 gallon drums. Concentrated pear juice is a popular item in South America.

Fresh fruit packing continues but on a lesser footing as some orchardists, many with worn out trees, have pulled them up and converted the land to other uses. New techniques for orchard maintenance and development are in place. An example is that in some orchards, new trees are planted closer together on the older tracts thus, while the orchard acreage is not growing, there are more trees per acre. The major soft fruit crop is pears: Bartlett, bosc and comice. Peaches and apples follow at a distance.

In early springtime, when temperatures sometimes dip below a critical point, signals send "smudge crews," mostly school kids grades 8 through 12, boys and some girls, nearly 1,000 of them (with special "smudging" work permits), into the orchards around 4 a.m. In years past, crews hand-light pots of oil to heat the air around the trees to keep the pear buds from freezing.

Pears are packed in boxes, weighed, then shipped to distant buyers

---

"All This '*Gluck*' in the Air"

With red eyes, hacking cough, and singed fingers, her son came home from smudging looking like a London chimney sweep.

— from *Oregon Journal*. May 19, 1970. Refer to bibliography

As the almost no wind moved the dense, suffocating, black smoke from the burning oil throughout the Rogue Valley, Medford, would be "smoked in" from the flaming pots.

Who Goes There ?

Early morning street cleaning crews are seen out with the tank truck washing Medford streets, yet the smudge is so think they drive with their lights on.

— from *Oregon Journal*. May 20, 1970. Refer to bibliography

There are no more open oil pots. But there are improved heating pots, which nobody really wants to talk about because agricultural heating is exempt from the air-quality environmental rules. Many orchardists converted their smoking, stinking, pots to similar looking propane burners – less cost to operate and far less pollution. In some orchards, large fans keep the air stirred while other orchards have overhead sprinklers to protect the buds. But there are still smudge pots in many orchards, although modernized pots have re-breathers in an attempt to minimize pollution. At the present time, there are no commercial orchards within Medford's city limits but the fruit industry is still a paramount contributor to Medford's economy. ◇

13

Medford:
A City in the State of Jefferson?

A uniqueness, that ties in with the "isolation" of the Medford area from the rest of the state, was an effort some years ago by people in several southern Oregon counties (Coos, Curry, Douglas, Josephine, Jackson, Klamath), to "divorce" themselves from Oregon. They sought to form the State of Jefferson. Californians in Del Norte and Siskiyou counties bordering Oregon were a part of the plan.

(Modoc County, California had an interest but it petered out when a commotion in its back yard in "Surprise Valley" no less, bordering Nevada, petitioned to join Nevada – not Jefferson.)

The complaint from a vocal portion of these dual-state, multi-county populations, had to do with their claim of being ignored by their state governments for such as road improvements and other issues. The common cry from each of these counties centered around an effort to secede and form a new state – Jefferson. By declaration, these counties would secede every Thursday until they got the attention they felt was lacking.

Of many peeves was when driving between Medford and Brookings, both in Oregon, the highway dipped into California for a way then crossed back into Oregon. Border residents had complained for over 40 years about unnecessary delays in their daily border commuting of being forced to pass through "California Customs" – the bug inspections.

On November 27, 1941 there appeared a "Proclamation of Independence of patriotic rebellion against Oregon and California to secede each Thursday until the indifferent state governments started road building and answered other long standing issues. Highway 99 was "seized" and copies of the proclamation

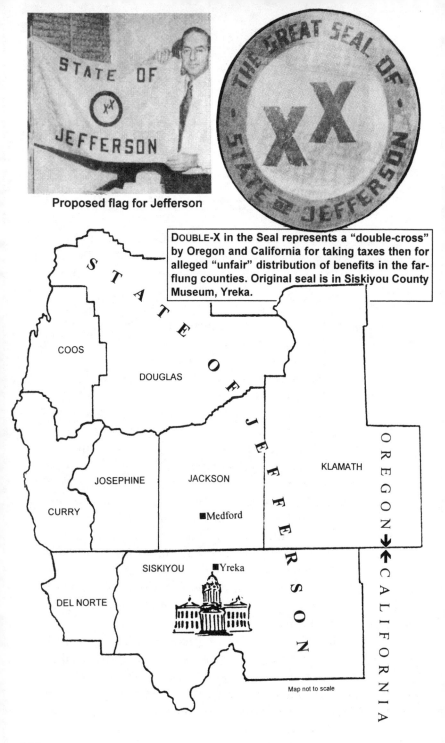

Proposed flag for Jefferson

DOUBLE-X in the Seal represents a "double-cross" by Oregon and California for taking taxes then for alleged "unfair" distribution of benefits in the far-flung counties. Original seal is in Siskiyou County Museum, Yreka.

THE GREAT SEAL OF · STATE OF JEFFERSON

XX

STATE OF JEFFERSON

COOS
DOUGLAS
JOSEPHINE
JACKSON
KLAMATH
CURRY
■Medford
SISKIYOU   ■Yreka
DEL NORTE
OREGON
CALIFORNIA

Map not to scale

were distributed to motorists as they "crossed state lines." Each motorist was given a red and blue windshield sticker reading

I HAVE VISITED JEFFERSON, THE 49TH STATE

The San Francisco *Examiner* sent a reporter. The New York *Times* ran a story. *Life Magazine* sent a photog and a writer who "sloshed through the mud" after a seasonal heavy rain, snapping pictures and talking with the "Jeffersonians."

The big public "declaration of independence" was planned for a Sunday morning. The various newspapers, wire services and newsreel companies had their cameramen and reporters assembled at Yerka for the big event as Yreka was to be the temporary state capitol.

The locals practiced their roles. An all-girl drum and bugle corps brassed and beat the air in rehearsal for the big day.

John L. Childs, 78, a retired jurist from Crescent City, was the new "Governor" of Jefferson. His inaugural speech included a paraphrase from I Kings XII:16:

When all Isreal saw the King gave them no confidence they cried, 'O King, what do we get.' We want you to know from now on the King can take care of himself and we of the State of Jefferson can take care of ourselves.

All was within mere hours of readiness, when the radio's of the nation blared forth with the news that the Japanese had attacked Pearl Harbor for it was December 7, 1941. The start of World War-II for the United States caused the secession movement to be squashed by the shear weight of the other event.

There was a flurry of excitement for forming the State of Jefferson in the early 1970's, but nothing on the scale of the flurry of the winter of 1941. Many citizens of these areas of both states still, in 1996, consider their respective state governments favor the more populous portions of the states and charge that each state still provides less attention to their "far flung" parts.

This was particularly true when it came to road improvements. Medford, as an example, was isolated not only by the serpentine highway between it and Portland, but by a granddaddy of a corkscrew highway between Medford and Yreka, California.

This latter is old Highway 99 that loosely parallels a free-

STATE OF JEFFERSON ?

HASKINS GARAGE

A severe peeve had to do with gasoline prices on the Oregon side of the mountain. The Model-T Ford had a 6 gallon gas tank and no one attempted to drive from Yreka to Medford for shopping (no sales tax in Oregon!), without carrying a spare can of gas due to the wicked road. Finally, on "landing" in Ashland, or going on into Medford, motorists were forced to pay what they termed "excessive" prices for gasoline especially if they had California license plates. "We had one of the few gas pumps in town in those days," declared Mr. Haskins at his garage and gas pump. "We would charge what we could get." The hope, if the State of Jefferson movement was successful, was to do something about the high price of gasoline.*

---

*Over seventy years later Medford gasoline prices are still "excessive," visitors complain, when compared to prices 30 miles farther up the road. (Ed.)

way over the Siskiyou Mountains. These old twisting roads are noted by their steepness and sharp turns with speeds on many curves restricted to about 20 miles per hour. When the post-war federal road-building boom came along and brought the freeway through the center of the area – Interstate 5 – the pressure for state-sponsored roads was relieved. If the freeway had not come along, who knows? – maybe all "Jeffersonians" would be taking Thursday's off! ◇

—14—
What's Happening in the Timber Business

Timber Products Company, formerly the Tomlin Box Company, began work in 1919. This was Medford's first sawmill. Until after World War-II the wood box business was firm, but cardboard cartons, costing users considerably less money, came into style and has all but ended the wood box business. Timber Products Company went into the veneer and plywood business in 1955, and later particle board which is made from tons of earlier discarded scraps.

The Medford Corporation (MEDCO), a sawmill and finishing plant which started on a 33 acre site that was enlarged to about 93 acres in later years, near the north Medford freeway interchange, started as the Brownlee-Olds Lumber Company in 1922. Finally, after various pressures on the timber business partially brought about by environmentalists, MEDCO shut down in 1989 putting hundreds out of work. Its equipment was sold and the mill was dismantled.

In 1973, a particle board plant under the name MEDITE was built and continues to operate nearby.

—For a comprehensive look at the timber industry, refer to bibliography for *This Is Logging and Sawmilling.*

Roxy Ann Peak
3,571 elev

Orchard

Hillcrest Orchard

← Rogue Valley Mem. Hospital

Murphy Road

Barnett Road

Rogue Valley
Country Club

St. Mary's High Sch. →

Rogue Valley Manor

Barneburg Hill

Interstate-5

Bear Creek

Photographed about 1972 by Bert Webber

The 10-story tall Rogue Valley Manor is easy to spot in this photograph made from a private airplane about 1972. By 1996, nearly the entire area of the photo, east of the freeway including about half-way up the near side of Roxie Ann Peak, has been developed.

15

Medford's Major Retirement Residence

It started as a dream in the mid-1950's but after opening its doors in January 1961, the Rogue Valley Manor, 35 years later, is well established and has already been through several expansions. One cannot miss seeing the Manor, with its over 200 apartments in a 10-story high-rise, for it is perched on more than 300 acres on top of Barneberg Hill in the southeast corner of Medford.

The Manor is such a landmark, that when aircraft traffic is a little thick, the joke is that incoming pilots are to "go do a few turns around the Manor" while they await landing clearance.

> There are about a dozen retirement and life-care communities in the Medford area of which the Rogue Valley Manor is the largest.

The Manor is a nonprofit community for active retired persons. This institution has become a complex, for in recent years an hillside of condominium-styles houses have been added. There is, in-house, a major health-care clinic.

The Manor's residents do not have to leave the premises unless they wish to do so as the facility offers many community services. These include an in-house shopping mall, banks, travel agency, dentist, pharmacy and just outside the door, the 9-hole Quail Point Golf Course and driving range.

Plans for the future include a 6-story high-rise apartment building adjacent to the main building. ◇

119

Southern Oregon Concert Band (formerly titled Southern Oregon Symphonic Band) offers free concerts during its September - June season in Medford and nearby cities. Concert pictured was in Lithia Park's Butler Band Shell in Ashland.

16

Medford is Blessed with Music
Choir, Symphony, Band, Community Concerts

Southern Oregon's oldest public choral organization, the Rogue Valley Choral, was founded in 1973 by some women who were interested in fine choral music. The first season, the Choral gave two concerts with its 38 members. On that program were Bach's "Komm, Jesu, Komm" and Respighi's "Laud to the Nativity." Since then, the group has grown to over 75 members.

Lynn Sjolund was the founding director of the Choral and has conducted it during all but three years of its existence. Those years he served as Director of Choral Activities at Loyola University of the South in New Orleans. He has degrees from the University of Oregon and did graduate study in Germany. He has served as President of the Oregon Music Educators Association and the Northwest Music Educators Association.

The Rogue Valley Choral has presented concerts and appeared with the Rogue Valley Symphony and the Britt Festival Orchestra on many occasions.

In 1993, the Choral traveled to Europe and was part of a festival in Veszprem, Hungary where they sang with a Veszprem choir and orchestra and with soloists from Budapest. They also sang in Austria and in the Czech Republic. In 1995 the members completed a successful tour in Sweden and in Norway where they performed before enthusiastic audiences.

Membership in the Rogue Valley Choral is by audition. The members come from wide backgrounds but all have experience singing in college, community, church or school choirs. Their traditional rehearsal period is at North Medford High School on Monday nights.

◇

The oldest and largest band in the region is the Southern Oregon Concert Band that got its start as a Shrine Band in 1909. Over the years, many dozens of men were part of the band. This was an award-winning, sharp-looking, quick-stepping uniformed marching band complete with Glockenspiel and Drum Major.

During the 1970's and 1980's, when enthusiasm for membership in fraternal orders declined, the band was unable to offer a balance of instrumentation as many of its older members were no longer able to do street marching.

By official invitation of the Shrine, which has its Temple in Ashland, men of the community who were not Masons, were invited to join the band. Although there was an immediate infusions of non-Mason adult musicians, there remained an imbalance in instrumentation. As an example, the band had lost all of its flutes and piccolos and many of its reeds. But there were many women flutists as well as other band-type women musicians in the community.

Would the Temple have difficulty if women joined this expanded band? The "official" Shrine Band, although small, still played for official functions. It was declared there was no conflict with the Charter. Accordingly, word seeped throughout the community that competent adult female musicians would be welcome. At this writing, approximately 45 percent of the members of the Southern Oregon Concert Band are women.

For about five years, this group of dedicated musicians played under the banner of the Southern Oregon Symphonic Band. But the Board of Control agreed with the director, John E. Drysdale, that while the band's repertoire included a wide variety of music, it was not truly "symphonic" thus the name was changed at the end of the 1995-1996 season.

John E. Drysdale holds baccalaureate and graduate degrees in music from the University of Oregon where he studied violin and French Horn as well as conducting. He was Concert Master in the University of Oregon Symphony (summers 1963, 1965) and he was Concert Master with the Rogue Valley Symphony and Guest Conductor (1964-1974). He was honored by the Northwest Bandmasters Association in 1978. His career saw him as teacher and director of orchestras in various schools including 24 years at Medford High School from which he retired in 1983. His school orchestras won many awards and honors. Drysdale was invited to direct the Southern Oregon Symphonic Band in 1990 and continues to the present time.

> **The Southern Oregon Concert Band is believed to be the only band of its size in Oregon where membership is open to any adult, without audition, who has undergone reasonable school or private instruction on a band instrument and who will seriously attend weekly rehearsals.**

The band presently has 64 active members with balanced instrumentation in all sections of the ensemble. Membership is primarily from Medford (46%) and Ashland (37%) and is sponsored by the Ashland Hillah Temple Shrine Band. It is supported by donations received from appreciative audiences, assistance from the Shrine German Band and from membership dues. The band's season is from September through early June.

<>

Medford began a new chapter in its cultural history at 8:15 p.m. on November 16, 1967, when conductor Frederick Palmer raised his baton to signal the first notes from the brand new Rogue Valley Symphony. The selection was Franz Schubert's "Rosamunde" Overture.

Two years earlier, Palmer arrived at Southern Oregon State College as Assistant Professor of Music. "I chose to work here because I very much wanted to found an orchestra and I thought this area would welcome live symphonic music, he said.

MarAbel Frohnmayer and the late Elmo Stevenson, then President of the college, agreed. Between them, they got the ball rolling. In two short years, funds were raised, musicians were recruited and with strong support from the college, Palmer's ambition became a reality.

The Rogue Valley Symphony began with 55 musicians and runs between 65 to 70 at the present writing. Palmer smiles as he recalls the uncanny good fortune he had in filling the positions in the early years. "When I sorely needed an oboe, somebody would call and apply for the position." The fledgling orchestra played four concerts a season with two performances of each program rotating among halls in Medford, Ashland and in Grants Pass.

Thirty years later, the Rogue Valley Symphony has become a major player in the region that is nationally known for the quality of its performing arts. Now led by Arthur Shaw, its first full-time director/conductor,

Mr. Shaw earned his Master's Degree in Conducting at Wichita State University in Kansas where he was Concert-Master of the university's orchestra. He did further study at the University of Michigan's International Master Course in Vienna. Arthur Shaw has achieved prominence in conducting in num-erous places including the New York Festival Orchestra.

The Rogue Valley Symphony's comprehensive season includes five subscription concerts, four seasonal Candlelight Concerts and two family concerts in Medford. The orchestra still plays in all three cities. Within the orchestra is a string quintet, the "Chamber Players." Each year this group entertains more than 7,500 young people in school classrooms.

<>

A Civic Music Association was formed in Medford in the 1930's which grew to become the Community Concerts. Each year, an intensive drive is made for memberships, the money collected used to meet fees and expenses of visiting musicians. The majority of memberships comes from renewals but there is usually room for some new members to replace normal attrition.

Visiting Entertainers

Many dozens of performers and companies have played in Medford. To name only a few would include Andre Segovia, Vienna Choir Boys, Mantovani, Itzak Perlman, Osipov Balalaika Orchestra from Moscow, Preservation Hall Band, New York Light Opera Company, Pittsburg Symphony Orchestra, Van Cliburn, Ray Charles, and the Imperial Chinese Acrobats.

The number of memberships is limited only by the number of seats available in the concert halls. In Medford's peak years, up to 2,000 persons, true concert lovers because of lack of air-conditioning and the hard school gymnasium bleachers that served as seats, held season tickets. Concerts are presently staged in either of the two high school auditoriums there being 800 seats in North Medford High School and 900 seats in South Medford High School. When the Craterian Ginger Rogers Theater construction is completed, the Community Concerts will plausibly be held there. <>

—Frank C. Clark, Architect—

The old Craterian Theater had a 1920's vaudeville stage with a grand Wurlitzer pipe organ. The show place was also a motion picture theater. The organ was sold many years ago then the show house was closed for a long time. At this writing the building is being totally reconstructed except for the corner wall along Central Avenue and Eighth Street.

Schoenstein Organ in First Presbyterian Church, Medford. (LOWER) Selected stop knobs.

126

Those Magnificent Sounds From Pipe Organs

It appears that Medford's churches were mostly piano and reed organ equipped until a salesman, James A. Bamford, representing the Reuter Organ Company of Lawrence, Kansas, hit the town early in the 1920's. Musically speaking, Medford has never been the same since.

For a city of its size, by the end of the 1920's Medford had at least four Reuter pipe organs. These were in the Baptist (1923), Methodist (1924), Presbyterian (1927) and Catholic (1928) churches. If there were others, they have not been discovered. Pipe organs come in such an unlimited variety of sizes and capabilities that to try to describe all of them would be a Herculean task let alone inappropriate for this book.

For newcomers to the sounds that emanate from an organ's pipes, listeners may sit in wonder but not have the slightest idea of what makes it all happen. But never mind what causes the sounds, just listen and enjoy.

One's first encounter with a pipe organ was probably in a church, or synagogue. On entering a sanctuary equipped with a large pipe organ, the wall of pipes behind the pulpit is immediately impressive, and when the pipes "speak," the sound can stir one's innermost soul. In some of the larger installations, the rumble of bass notes can shake a building.

The majority of churches have the keyboard (manual) in front of the audience as well as the pipes, but some installations the organ – console and pipes – may be in a balcony. In these churches, the organ can be heard but not seen, unless one cranes one's neck backward and upward. Whether the pipes are in front or in the back, one cannot tell which pipes are playing ("speaking") and which ones are just for display – silent ("dumb") – just by looking at them.

Before the advent of the so-called electronic organs in the early 1930's, if a church had an organ it was either a reed or a pipe organ. The reed models (in the days before radio-tubed amplifiers), lacked the power of pipe organs but large reed organs were found in many churches. A number of the churches in Medford had them. There were "Parlor" models in small churches. These little piano-size, foot-powered pump organs were also in thousands in homes across the country. For their period in history, the little reeds were as popular as today's electronic keyboards. Today these 19th and early 20th century reed organs are collectors' items and are mostly found in museums.

Pipe organs, at least the larger ones, have always been looked upon as something majestic and were found in mid-size and larger churches. But the degree of "majesty" was shared by the competence of the organist, not in the organ alone The great cathedrals often had one or more pipe organs. *

Lindbergh Compares B-24 Bomber to a Pipe Organ

I was taking every opportunity to familiarize myself with the B-24 heavy bomber that we would be building at the new Ford Motor Company's Willow Run, Michigan plant during World War II. The actual flying of the ship is simple enough, but the secondary controls, instruments, switches, radio, hydraulic system, electrical system, etc., etc., remind me of a pipe organ.

I find the best way to get to know a new airplane, or a new pipe organ, is to spend as much time as possible at either, along with a study of the design, its performance specifications and operating instructions.

—Based on *The Wartime Journals of Charles A. Lindbergh* p.638. See bibliography.

A word needs be said about the pipe organ that was in the Craterian Theater in downtown Medford. Theater pipe organs do not relate to church pipe organs because of a different choice of the voices – stops. The Wurlitzer theater organs lost their popu-

---

* In Southern Oregon, the only facility with two pipe organs is Southern Oregon State College in Ashland.

larity with the advent of sound motion pictures. In the so-called "good-old days," nimble-fingered Wurlitzer organists supplied musical and some unconventional sounds as they accompanied silent movies. The Craterian's organ was sold and removed many years ago and was last reported to be in a private residence in the Portland area.

Although there are numerous private residences sporting pipe organs in the larger cities, a number of the organs having been salvaged from old theaters, there are no known pipe organs in homes in Medford at the present time.

On June 18, 1923, the Rev. F. R. Leach of the First Baptist Church sent a letter of transmittal to the Reuter Organ Company of Lawrence, Kansas. The attached papers included a signed contract, a check for $955.00 as the down payment on a pipe organ, and the specifications to which the organ was to be constructed. The minister pointed out:

As building is expected to be completed by Sept. 1st. desire the organ installed during the building period. If there is anything you desire done while building, inform me.

Reuter organ, First Baptist Church

The specifications had been written by the traveling salesman who knew his product and was an expert when it came to
convincing congregations that they needed to buy a pipe organ
to enhance their worship services.

The organ will be two manuals and pedal.
Compass of the manuals CC to C4   61 notes
Compass of pedals CCC to G   32 notes

GREAT ORGAN

1. 8 ft.	Open Diapason	Metal	73 pipes
2. 8 ft.	Dulciana	Metal	73 pipes
3. 8 ft.	Melodia	Wood & metal	73 pipes
4. 4 ft.	Flute d'Amour	Wood	73 pipes

5. Swell to Great   4 ft.
6. Swell to Great   8 ft.
7. Swell to Great 16 ft.
8. Great to Great   4 ft.
9. Great to Great 16 ft.
10. Great Unison Off

SWELL ORGAN

11. 8 ft.	Open Diapason	Metal	73 pipes
12. 8 ft.	Salicional	Metal	73 pipes
13. 8 ft.	Aeoline	Metal	73 pipes
14. 8 ft.	Stopped Diapason	Wood	73 pipes
15. 4 ft.	Flute Harmonic	Metal	73 pipes
16. 8 ft.	Oboe	Metal	73 pipes
17. -	Tremolo–	–	–

18. Swell to Swell   4 ft.
19. Swell to Swell 16 ft.
20. Swell Unison Off

PEDAL ORGAN

21. 16 ft.	Bourdon	Wood		32 pipes
22. 16 ft.	Lieblich Gedeckt	Wood	From #14	32 pipes

23. Swell to Pedal   8 ft.
24. Great to Pedal   8 ft.

COMBINATION MOVEMENTS

Operated by pistons under their respective manuals.
Adjustable at keyboard and visibly affecting stop keys.

ACCESSORIES

27. Balanced Expression Pedal controlling entire organ
28. Balances Crescendo Pedal
29. Great to Pedal reversible
30. Crescendo Indicator
31. Organist's Bench
32. A Centrifugal Electric Blower and Generator Outfit
33. Detached Console placed to suit purchaser

Note: A separate rank was installed for 2 ²/3 ft. Flute in January 1996

– 0 –

When a professional salesman gets an order, it's only in the movies that he celebrates and takes the next several days off.

Reuter's man stayed in town ringing doorbells on various churches to see if he could scare up some more business. In other words, he "worked the town" just like traveling encyclopedia and vacuum cleaner salesmen do. The only difference: He did not have a product in hand for he was peddling pipe organs.

Just when he signed the Methodist Episcopal Church is unclear but records reveal that an Organ Committee, including the pastor, studied propositions from several companies. The pastor made a special trip of investigation then the committee and Official Board of the church decided upon the Reuter. It seems likely that the committee visited the Baptist church, a few blocks away, to listen to and study the new Reuter installed there just weeks earlier.

One needs to bear in mind that buying a pipe organ is not merely signing an order then a little later here comes the delivery truck and all one does is move the instrument into the church, plug the power cord into a socket then sit down and play an hymn. It is true that some pipe organs can be pretty small, about the size of an overgrown piano, but the specifications for these fairly large church organs often required severe modifications to the building into which it was to fit. While this was being done, Reuter would build an organ to the specifications agreed upon. As we saw with the Baptists, the Methodists also had a building being constructed so they merely modified the plans to accommodate a new pipe organ. The members decided to have the Reuter Organ Company build an instrument for them and place

—Methodist Church Archives

(TOP) **Methodist Church as it appeared, new, in 1923.**
(LOWER) **In 1966. (Building appears to be leaning due
to optical distortion.)**

132

it in the chambers shown in a changed blue print dated November 20, 1923.

The Methodists have had a long and distinguished history in the Rogue River Valley. They built the first church in Jacksonville (which is still stranding but now used by another denomination) in 1854, although the Methodists founded their congregation there in 1853.

> **Mrs. Jane Carrol was for many years a devoted and benevolent member of the congregation. In her will she provided $5,000 specifically for the building fund then she made the church the residuary legatee of her estate. The total of her benefactions amounting to approximately $14,000. As a fitting tribute to her devotion, the Official Board voted unanimously to make the fine new organ "The Jane Carrol Memorial Organ."**

The new building, with Reuter Pipe Organ, which cost about $105,000 including the organ, was dedicated on Sunday, July 13, 1924. That night there was a special recital – the first public pipe organ concert in Medford. A newspaper clipping reveals:

Included in the program at the Methodist Church tonight, given my Mrs. Lynch are both sacred and secular numbers making the recital the first of its nature to be heard in Medford. The most ambitious are the Sonata by Barowski

Programme

First Sonata for Organ	Felix Borowsk (*sic*)
Allegro Von Troppo	
Andante	
Allegro con fuoco	
Mrs. Lynch	
The Lost Chord	Arthur Sullivan
Mr. James Stevens	
Barcarolle in E Minor	William Faulkes
In Moonlight	Ralph Kinder
Narcissus	Ethelbert Nevin
Grand Processional March	Gounod
(From the Queen of Sheba)	
Mrs. Lynch	
Evensong	Edward Johnson
A Southern Fantasy	Ernest F. Hawke
Largo from New World Symphony	Doorak (*sic.*)

—*Medford Mail Tribune* - July 14 1924

and Processional March of Gounod, heard at "The Welfarer." The Largo from the New World Symphony, one of the most beautiful compositions in all musical literature, Nevin's poetic "Narcissus," and a "Southern Fantasy" where the melodies of "Old Black Joe" and "Dixie" are played simultaneously are sure to please all tastes. To the piano or organ student, a recital of this type is an invaluable education. The organ itself possessed a sufficient variety of speaking stops to be capable of many orchestral effects.

Specifications of a
Reuter Electro-Pneumatic Pipe Organ
for
First Methodist Episcopal Church, Medford, Oregon.

The organ was to be two manuals and pedal.
Compass of the manuals CC to C4   61 notes
Compass of pedals CCC to G   32 notes

GREAT ORGAN

1. 8 ft.	Open Diapason	Metal	73 pipes
2. 8 ft.	Dulciana	Metal	73 pipes
3. 8 ft.	Melodia	Wood	73 pipes
4. 8 ft.	Doppel Flute	Wood	73 pipes
5 8 ft.	Gamba	Metal	73 pipes
6. 4 ft.	Flute d'Armour	W & M	73 pipes
7.	Chimes		20 tubes

8. Swell to Great   4 ft.
9. Swell to Great   8 ft.
10. Swell to Great   16 ft.
11. Swell to Great   4 ft.
12. Great to Great   16 ft.
13. Great Unison Off

SWELL ORGAN

14. 16 ft.	Bourdon	Wood	73 pipes
15. 8 ft.	Diapason	Metal	73 pipes
16. 8 ft.	Salicional	Metal	73 pipes
17. 8 ft.	Aeoline	Metal	73 pipes
18. 8 ft.	Stopped Diapason	Wood	73 pipes
19. 8 ft.	Vox Celeste	Metal	73 pipes
20. 4 ft.	Flute Harmonic	Metal	73 pipes
21. 8 ft.	Vox Humana	Reed	73 pipes
22. 8 ft.	Oboe	Reed	73 pipes
23.	Tremolo		

24. Swell to Swell   4 ft.
25. Swell to Swell 16 ft.
26. Swell Unison Off

PEDAL ORGAN

27. 16 ft. Bourdon	Wood	44 pipes
28. 16 ft. Lieblich Gedeckt	Wood (from No. 14)	32 notes
29. 8 ft. Flute	Wood (from No. 27)	32 notes
30. 8 ft. Violincello	Metal (from No. 5)	32 notes

31. Great to Pedal 8 ft.
32. Swell to Pedal 8 ft.
    Swell to Pedal 4 ft.

COMBINATION MOVEMENTS

Operated by pistons under their respective manuals.
Adjustable ay keyboard and visibly affecting Stop Keys.

33. Six, acting on Great and Pedal Organs and their respective couplers.
34. Six, acting on Swell and Pedal Organs and their respective couplers
35. Six, master pistons acting on entire organ.

ACCESSORIES

36. Balanced Great Pedal	37. Balance Swell Pedal
38. Balanced Crescendo Pedal	39. Great to Pedal Reversible
40. Sfortzando Reversible	41. Sfortzando Indicator
42. Crescendo Indicator	43. Organist's Bench

44. A Centrifugal Electric Blower and Generator Outfit
45. Detached Console as desired   (Organ placed in special built chamber)

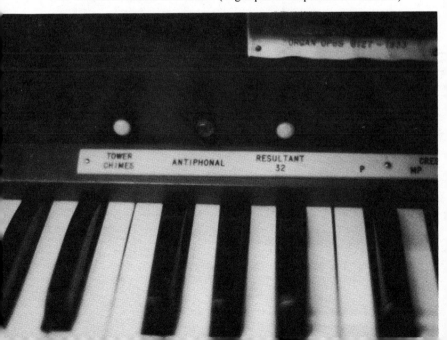

(PAGE 135) **Section of great manual with part of manufacturer's plate showing this Moller console was made in 1933.** (ABOVE) **Organist Linda McGuire playing a Postlude during a Sunday service. Records of the First United Methodist Church reveal that the present console, a Moller (*Opus* 6127) built in 1933, was purchased in March 1980 from the First Baptist Church of Bakersfield, California. It replaced the original Reuter* console.** (LOWER) **Selected stops on the Moller.**

— 0 —

As we have seen, the Baptists, Methodists, and the Presbyterians (to be discussed shortly) had new pipe organs. Some say the Roman Catholics had noticed the publicity that went with the

---

*The Methodist Church in Ashland bought a Reuter Pipe Organ in 1929. Its console was traded for a Moller in 1987 then the system was further modified in 1989 and is currently operating. The Methodist Church in Coos Bay also has a Reuter.

inauguration of new pipe organs so a faction in the parish decided to investigate what it would take for their church to also acquire a pipe organ. Details are lacking but on the heals of the Presbyterian installation, Reuter's Mr. Jost, the installer, called on the Rev. Fr. Francis W. Black at Church of the Nativity (later renamed Sacred Heart Catholic Church).

On September 2, 1928, Fr. Black sent a letter to Reuter Organ Company ordering "your $6,500 (2 manual) organ" but he did not give any specifications as he was apparently looking at a catalog. The priest wrote: "[we] trust you will have it installed by Dec. 1st or at least before Christmas." The company immediately sent a telegram to him confirming his order and at the same time, fired off another telegram to its regional salesman in Portland, James A. Bamford. The salesman was to take the next train to Medford and look up Father Black.

Reuter's man met with Fr. Black to arrange a regular purchasing contract and to be certain of the specifications for the organ and that the balcony, where Fr. Black wanted it, would be ready. This was for the present church which was then under construction.

Sacred Heart Catholic Church

REVEREND FRANCIS W. BLACK

CHURCH OF THE NATIVITY
MEDFORD, OREGON

Sept 2, 1928

Reuter Organ Co,
Lawrence, Kan.,

Dear Sirs,

Several weeks ago, Mr. Jost, your president, spoke to me about installing a pipe-organ in our new church, now under construction.

$1500 (2 manual) I now place the order for your organ, and trust you will have it installed by Dec 1st or at latest before Christmas.

Mr. Jost discussed the matter with our architect and also suggested that the pipes follow the circle of our rose window. This will be pleasing to us.

The organ will be paid for in full upon complete installation. Kindly let us hear from you at an early date.

P.S. H balcony will not be ready until Nov.

Yours truly,
F. W. Black, Pastor

Reuter organ, Sacred Heart Catholic Church

138

Specifications of a
Reuter Electro-Pneumatic Pipe Organ
for
Sacred Heart Catholic Church, Medford, Oregon.

Two manual and Pedal

MANUALS	Compass CC to C4 – 61 notes
Pedals	Compass CCC to G – 32 notes
Action	Electro-Pneumatic
Registration	Controlled by Stop Keys
Console	Detached
Casing	None except console
Display pipes	None
Organ chambers	To be built in and finished by purchaser in accordance with plans and specifications furnished by the Reuter Organ Company

GREAT ORGAN

1.	8 ft.	Diapason	metal	73 pipes
2.	8 ft.	Claribel Flute	Wood	73 pipes
3.	8 ft.	Viol d'Gamba	Metal	73 pipes
4.	8 ft.	Dulciana	Metal	73 piped
5.	8 ft.	Tuba	Reed	73 pipes
6.	4 ft.	Octave	Metal	73 pipes
7.	4 ft.	Flute Traverso	Wood and Metal	61 notes
7½		Blank stop (preparation only) (chimes)		

COUPLERS TO GREAT:

8. Great to Great   4 ft.
9. Great to Great 16 ft.
10. Great Unison Off
11. Swell to Great   4 ft.
12. Swell to Great   8 ft.
13. Swell to Great 16 ft.

SWELL ORGAN

14.	16 ft. Bourdon	Wood	97 pipes
15.	8 ft. Diapason	Metal	73 pipes
16.	8 ft. Gedeckt	Wood	73 pipes
17.	8 ft. Salicional	Metal	73 pipes
18.	8 ft. Vox Celeste	Metal	61 pipes
19.	8 ft. Orchestral Horn	Synthetic	73 notes

20. 4 ft.	Flauto Dolce	Wood and Metal	73 notes
21. 2 ⅔ ft.	Nasard (*sic*)	Wood and Metal	61 notes
22. 2 ft.	Flautino	Wood and Metal	61 notes
23. 8 ft.	Oboe	Reed	73 pipes
24	Tremolo		
24½	Black stop (preparation only) (Vox Humana)		

COUPLERS TO SWELL

25. Swell to Swell   4 ft.
26. Swell to Swell   16 ft.
27. Swell Unison Off

PEDAL ORGAN

28. 32 ft.	Resultant		32 notes
29. 16 ft.	Bourdon (Extra large)	Wood	32 pipes
30. 16 ft.	Lieblich Gedeckt	Wood	32 notes
31. 8 ft.	Dolce Flute	Wood	32 notes
32. 8 ft.	Trombone	Reed	32 notes
32½	Black stop (preparation only)		

COUPLERS TO PEDAL

33. Great to Pedal   8 ft.
34. Swell to Pedal   8 ft.
35. Swell to Pedal   4 ft.

COMBINATION MOVEMENTS
Operated by pistons under their respective Manuals.
Adjustable at Keyboard and visibly affecting Stop Keys.

36. Six acting on Great and pedal Organs and their couplers
37. Six acting on Swell and Pedal Organs and their couplers

ACCESSORIES

38. Balanced Expression Swell-Pedal
38a Balanced Crescendo Pedal
39. Balanced Expression Swell Pedal
40. Great to Pedal Reversible
41. Crescendo Indicator
42. Organist's bench
43. Organ Blower
44. Key action generator directly connected to blower.

As frequently occurs in selling, one sale leads to another. This occurred when the Methodists sought a pipe organ after the Baptists broke the ice. Then the publicity about the Presbyterian pipe organ sold another one to the Catholics in Medford then one to the Methodists in Ashland. There was a further spin-off to Grants Pass where St. Ann's Catholic church sent an order almost duplicating the Sacred Heart installation. The major difference being that Sacred Heart had a 8 ft. tuba on the GREAT manual and St. Ann's organ substitutes an 8 ft. Clarinet. Otherwise, says C. R. "Bob" Lewis, the organ technician who services most of the pipe organs in the region, these two Reuter organs are identical.

-0-

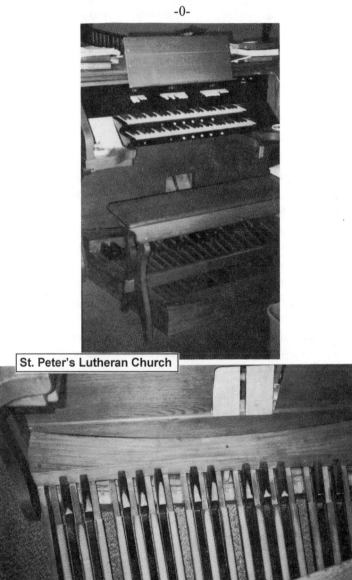

St. Peter's Lutheran Church

St. Peters Lutheran Church
(Limited information)

Reuter   2 manual
Year acquired unknown

GREAT		SWELL	
8 ft.	Open Diapason	8 ft.	Stopped Flute
4 ft.	Octave Diapason (separate rank)	8 ft.	Salicional
8 ft.	Dulciana	4 ft.	Viol Celeste
		4 ft.	Harmonic Flute

PEDAL
16   ft.Bourdon 32 note separate
8   ft.Open Diapason
Swell to Pedal
Great to Swelll

–0–

Zion Lutheran Church was built in 1927 but what was used to accompany congregational singing at that time has not been determined. Immediately following the close of World War-II, a fund raising drive was launched to acquire a pipe organ. To what lengths a study may have been made to determine what specifications to request, and which manufacturer to contract with, is elusive. The goal of the congregation was to bring in $4,000. This goal was met.This appears to be a reasonable sum for a substantial down payment on a pipe organ in this period. A detailed specification sheet has not been found but the organ pur-chased was a 2 manual Moller that had built in 1947.

Opus 7535

GREAT		SWELL	
8 ft.	Open Diapason	16 ft.	Bourdon
8 ft.	Salicional	8 ft.	Gedeckt
8 ft.	Flute	8 ft.	Salicional
4 ft.	Fugara	4 ft.	Salicional
4 ft.	Octave	4 ft.	Viole
		4 ft.	Flute
		4 ft.	Fugara
		2 $^2/_3$ ft.	Flute
		2 $^2/_3$ ft.	Fugara
		2 $^2/_3$ ft.	Viole 12th
		2 ft.	Flute
		2 ft.	Flautino
			Tremolo

Moller organ, Zion Lutheran Church

<u>PEDAL</u>

16 ft.	Bourdon
8 ft.	Flute
8 ft.	Open Diapason
4 ft.	Octave

<u>COUPLERS</u>
Great to Pedal
Swell to Pedal
Swell to Crescendo
Crescendo specifics: P / MP / MF / F

–0–

In February of 1992, a Bond Mechanical Action Pipe Organ was installed at St. Marks Episcopal Church.

This pipe organ contains 19 ranks (953 speaking pipes) in two manual divisions and a pedal division. This is a tracker action, meaning the connection between each key to the pipe is mechanical, differing from electro-pneumatic actions on other organs in Medford. Of the several uniquenesses of this organ are the two double draw stopknobs in which one sound is heard in the halfway position, and a more complex sound is heard when

Bond Tracker-action organ, St. Marks Episcopal Church

Bond Tracker-action organ, St. Marks Episcopal Church

the knob is pulled to its entire length. Also unique are the keys.

The white keys are made from cow bone and the blacks are of ebony. The pedals are oak and ebony.

SPECIFICATIONS

Manual Compass: C1 – G56
Pedal Compass: C1 – G32

GREAT

8 ft.	Principal	56 pipes in facade
8 ft.	Rohrflote	56 pipes
4 ft.	Octave	56 pipes
2 ²/₃ ft.	Quinte	from Sesquialtera
2 ft.	Superoctave	from Mixture
IV	Mixture	224 pipes *
II	Sesquialterea	112 pipes **
8 ft.	Trumpet	56 pipes

SWELL

8 ft.	Gedackt	56 pipes
8 ft.	Gemshorn	44 pipes, 1-12 common with Gedacckt
4 ft.	Koppelflote	56 pipes
2 ft.	Doublet	56 pipes
8 ft.	Krummhorn	56 pipes
		Tremolo

16 ft.	Sub Bass	32 pipes
8 ft.	Principal	30 pipes 1-2 common with Gt Principal 8 ft.
4 ft.	Choral Bass	31 pipes, 1 common with Great Octave 4 Ft.
16 ft.	Fagott	32 pipes

COUPLERS

| Great to Pedal | Swell to Pedal | Swell to Great |

ACCESSORIES

0.45 horsepower blower features 3 $5/8$ inch wind pressure
Organist's bench

---

* In mid-position plays the 2 ft. Superoctive. In fully drawn position plays Mixture IV.
** In mid-position this stop plays the Quinte 2 $2/3$ ft.. In fully drawn position plays the Sesquialtera II.

–0–

The Presbyterian Church in Southern Oregon got its start in Jacksonville when the Rev. Moses Williams founded a church there in 1857. Although Rev. Williams lived in Ashland, he also formed Presbyterian churches in Phoenix, Ashland, Eagle Point and in Medford. On March 29, 1885, just one month after the town was incorporated, he started the Presbyterian Church in Medford with nine charter members. The first services were held in the town's only school which was a one room affair at Ninth Street and South Central.

Jacksonville's influential banker, C. C. Beekman, who had a large part in the founding of Medford, donated some of his lots, at the corner of Holly and Main Streets, to "Father" Williams. Rev. Williams had this nick-name because of his elegant beard, not usually found among the Presbyterian clergy. A church building was completed and occupied on September 4, 1887. Regrettably, it burned to the ground only eight years later – October 15, 1895. Its next building was of brick. It was dedicated on Sunday, May 31, 1896.

The Presbyterian calling reached over a wide area and the congregation grew substantially to where a larger building was required. Mrs. Rebecca Finney donated some property one block south at Holly and 8th Streets.

The new building was ready for use in 1927 and a new three manual and pedal Reuter electro-pneumatic pipe organ had been installed. Its use was inaugurated with a concert on September 11, 1927, when Professor John Stark Evans, Assistant Dean of the School of Music, University of Oregon, was the guest organist. He played to an overflow audience numbering about 1,000.

After serving for thirty years, the Reuter Organ was in need of major overhaul or replacement. The Reid Organ Company of Santa Clara, California, supplied a new console in 1961 which was adapted to the Reuter wind chests and pipes.

When it was decided to remodel the sanctuary in 1972, the direction of the sanctuary was to be reversed which would require the dismantling of the organ. To help decide the fate of the organ, overhaul it or replace it, a special recital was offered by Professor Gayle Enger of the Music staff of Lewis and Clark College. He performed a wide variety of music therefore testing every capability of the organ.

The decision was made to keep it and fix it. Every piece of the organ was stored during the remodeling then reinstalled. During the years, three additional combination actions had been installed to improve the instrument's potential.

By 1987, it was determined that the old organ, now an amalgamation of parts from various manufacturers, was wearing out. The Session of the church weighed the question of rebuild – again – or replace. The decision was to look carefully for a replacement so, an Organ committee was selected to research the matter. In all, seven organ builders were considered. The committee traveled throughout Washington, Oregon and Northern California where they listened to and played* many pipe organs. After their study was completed, the Committee announced a unanimous recommendation in favor of having the Schoenstein Company of San Francisco build an organ for the church.

For over 64 years, the Reuter Pipe Organ helped lead generations of Presbyterians in worship, accompanied soloists and choirs and served as a solo instrument. The organ was ready to be retired.

---

* Within the committee were two experienced church organists, Virginia Peterson and Linda McGuire.

The George and Agnes Flanagan Pipe Organ

Medford's largest pipe organ is the George and Agnes Flanagan Schoenstein Electro-Pneumatic System™ (*Opus* 117) pipe organ in the First Presbyterian Church at 8th and Holly Streets.

It was installed during the early weeks of 1992 then the dedication service and first of eight public recitals was held on Sunday, May 10, 1992. Dr. Wilbur Russell, Organist, Choir Director and Instructor in church music at San Francisco Theological Seminary, San Anselmo, California, presented the first recital. The following seven recitals extended over a period of eight months with each designed to show different uses and properties of the organ. The final program on Saturday, December 12, was called "Children's 'Meet the Organ' Concert."

Dedication Concert – May 10, 1992

Prelude and Fugue in D   Buxtehude (1637 - 1707)

Concerto After Signor Meck   Walther (1684 - 1748)
    (Allegro   Adagio   Allegro)

Six Pieces for a Mechanical Clock Organ   CPE Bach (1714 - 1788)

Toccota in E   Krebs (1730 - 1780)

Passacaglia and Fugue in C Minor   JS Bach (1685 - 1750)

"Our God, Our Help in Ages Past" (Congregational Hymn)
        Text: Watt 1719. Tube: St. Anne 1708.

Fugue in E. Flat (St. Anne)   JS Bach

Two Chorales (From Eleven Chorale Preludes *Opus* 121)
    Blessed Ye, Who Live in Faith Unswerving
    O World, I Now Must Leave Thee

Praeludium Circulare   Widor (1845 – 1937)
    (Second Organ Symphony, *Opus* 13, No. 9)

Fantasy and Fugue on B/A/C/H   Liszt (1811 - 1886)

Specifications of a 3 Manual and Pedal
Schoenstein Electro-Pneumatic Detached Console
Schoenstein Pipe Organ for the
First Presbyterian Church, Medford, Oregon

GREAT
(Manual II – 3½" wind)

16 ft.	Salicional
8 ft.	Principal
8 ft.	Harmonic Flute
8 ft.	Bourdon
8 ft.	Salicional
4 ft.	Octave
4 ft.	Forest Flute
2 ²/₃ ft.	Quint
2 ft.	Super Octave
2 ft.	Chorus Mixture (*IV Ranks*)
8 ft.	Tromba
8 ft.	Clarinet
	Chimes

SWELL
(Manual III – enclosed – 4" wind)

8 ft.	Principal
8 ft.	Silver Flute
8 ft.	Viola
8 ft.	Celeste (*FF*)
4 ft.	Principal
4 ft.	Lieblich Gedeckt
2 ft.	Harmonic Piccolo
2 ft.	Fill Mixture (*III-V Ranks*)
16 ft.	Bassoon
8 ft.	Trumpet
8 ft.	Oboe
	Tremulant
	Swell 16 ft.
	Swell Unison Off
	Swell 4 ft.

SOLO
(Manual I – enclosed – 4½" wind)

8 ft.	Diapason
8 ft.	Bourdon (Wood)
4 ft.	Gemshorn
4 ft.	Chimney Flute
4 ft.	Forest Flute
2 ²/₃ ft.	Nazard
2 ft.	Flautino
1 ³/₅ ft.	Tierce (*TC*)
2 ft.	Chorus Mixture (*IV Ranks*)
8 ft.	Tromba
8 ft.	Clarinet
	Tremulant
	Solo Unison Off
	Solo 4 ft.
	Cymbelstern

PEDAL
(3½" and 5" wind)

32 ft.	Bourdon
16 ft.	Principal (*Wood and Metal*)
16 ft.	Salicional
16 ft.	Bourdon (*Wood*)
8 ft.	Octave
8 ft.	Flute
8 ft.	Bourdon
4 ft.	Super Octave
4 ft.	Flute
16 ft.	Trombone
16 ft.	Bassoon
8 ft.	Trumpet
4 ft.	Clarinet

COUPLERS

Great to Pedal	8 ft.		Solo to Great	16 ft.
Swell to Pedal	8 ft.		Solo to Great	8 ft.
Swell to Pedal	4 ft.		Solo to Great	4 ft.
Solo to Pedal	8 ft.		Swell to Solo	16 ft.
Swell to Great	16 ft.		Swell to Solo	8 ft.
Swell to Great	8 ft.		Swell to Solo	4 ft.
Swell to Great	4 ft.			

Solid State Capture Combination Action with
10 memories - 28 Pistons and toe studs
4 coupler reversibles   Full organ reversible
Crescendo pedal

Virginia Derickson Peterson
Organist
First Presbyterian Church

Since the first pipe organ was installed at First Presbyterian Church in 1927, many organists have served. The present organist arrived in Medford in 1960 as a public school music teacher and was immediately hired as substitute organist. She became organist at the first service in 1961, Sunday, January 1. With the exception of time out to have a family, Virginia Peterson has served as the regular organist for the church since that time.

She has studied with L. Stanley Glarum at Lewis and Clark College and attended workshops presented by Wilbur Russell, Lee Garrett, Joyce Jones and Marilyn Mason. She is a member of the American Guild of Organists and of the Presbyterian Association of Musicians.

Medford Parks Serve Unique Purposes
The "Sewer City Short Line" Railroad

Many acres of Medford parks serve a multitude of purposes from sit-on-a-bench-and-read to tennis courts, play or nap on the grass, go swimming, or take a free ride on a railroad.

In addition to the centrally located Hawthorne Park and Jackson Park, and Alba Park across from the library and post office with its gazebo-stage for special events, there are many more as Bear Creek Park where public programs and concerts are held throughout the year.

Veteran's Memorial Park on the south end of town (highway 99) has been carefully developed with much input, patience and hard work largely by the veterans themselves. It is an easily accessible memorial to veterans of the wars.

There are many tennis courts and small neighborhood parks. A special highly enjoyed, "pint-size" park is in mid-town on the southeast corner of Main and Central. The lot once contained a commercial building that burned in the 1970's. Rather than rebuild, the property was donated to the city for a "mini-park." This street-corner park with its benches, has become a resting place for shoppers who are sheltered on hot summer days by large shade trees. But the most amazing park – a one-of-a-kind anywhere, is the Medford Railroad Park.

Here is the only known city park in the nation where the public can get a free ride on a railroad. This occurs on alternate weekends in summer. The railroad's name, "Sewer City Short Line," is a catchy title for the 7½-inch gauge railroad operated by volunteer members of the Southern Oregon Live Steamers, a club of railroad enthusiasts in Medford and in the surrounding

(TOP) **Veterans Memorial Park is on South Pacific Highway near Stewart Street, adjacent from National Guard Armory.** (LOWER) **Swimming pool at Jackson Park.**

MEDCO 4-spot Willamette (TOP) logging locomotive in the woods near Butte Falls. (LOWER) The 4-spot is on display at the Medford Railroad Park, is the only locomotive of its type in Oregon.

VISITING THE 4-SPOT-MEDFORD

Each Engineer makes countless trips around the layout each run day. Jerry Hellinga's train illustrates the variety of passengers who come for a day's outing at Medford Railroad park.

area. A similar club, the Southern Oregon Chapter of the National Railway Historical Society, and a third group, the Rogue Valley Model Railroad Club are likewise active there.

It all started in 1959 when Medford Corporation (MEDCO) presented their Willamette logging locomotive to the City of Medford for public display. Jackson Park, in west Medford, was the chosen site. The Willamette rested there on a short length of track for many years and was climbed upon my hundreds of kids and adults alike. But, over the years, there was also vandalism.

The Pacific Northwest Chapter of the national organization tried to obtain the locomotive and move it to Portland. It was then that the "dander" was raised by Medford rail enthusiasts who formed the local chapter and set about to keep the rare gear-driven logging locomotive in Medford. It is the only locomotive of its type in Oregon. The local club was successful.

The local members asked the city for property on which a permanent historical railroad park might be built. The Willamette (also called a "side-winder") would be moved there. In time, the city agreed and offered the club a choice of several parcels. The rail historians accepted the use of some acreage near the

**Passengers waiting
for departure from
MacKenzie Station**

Safety is the No. 1 concern at the Medford Railroad Park.
Conductor Don Razey wears FM radio that all engineers and conductors use on trains of four or more cars. Conductors are at back of trains and are alert for passengers riding in a careless manner such as dragging feet, youngsters who "rock" the cars, etc. Conductor can order the train stopped when safety violation occurs – can put unruly passenger off trains.

156

Owner engineer Gus Young has just pulled away from MacKenzie Station, Medford Railroad Park, with her model SW-800 switcher heading a train.

North Medford freeway interchange where there were the remains of an obsolete and dismantled but completely cleaned up sewage plant. Thus the name for the railroad. Today the old "digester tank" is filled with granite for use as ballast on the park's tracks. The Live Steamers Club operates the Medford Railroad Park on an agreement with the city.

The main entry-way to the park is open every day, but the railroad part is open for free rides on the 2nd and 4th Sundays between May and September – weather permitting. The area is fenced for protection, has restrooms and good parking. People flock to the Railroad Park on operating days. The club members run up to seven people-carrying trains at a time thus the wait in line for a ride is never long.

Members of the "Steamers" build, own and operate a number of 7½-inch gauge locomotives. These engines weigh between 300 and 3,000 pounds and have values from about $12,000 to about $25,000 each. The locomotives are finished in the colors area. A similar club, the Southern Oregon Chapter of the National Railway Historical Society, and a third group, the Rogue Valley Model Railroad Club are likewise active there.

It all started in 1959 when Medford Corporation (MEDCO) presented their Willamette logging locomotive to the City of Medford for public display. Jackson Park, in west Medford, was the chosen site. The Willamette rested there on a short length of track for many years and was climbed upon my hundreds of kids and adults alike. But, over the years, there was also vandalism.

The Pacific Northwest Chapter of the national organization tried to obtain the locomotive and move it to Portland. It was then that the "dander" was raised by Medford rail enthusiasts who formed the local chapter and set about to keep the rare gear-driven logging locomotive in Medford. It is the only locomotive of its type in Oregon. The local club was successful.

The local members asked the city for property on which a permanent historical railroad park might be built. The Willamette (also called a "side-winder") would be moved there. In time, the city agreed and offered the club a choice of several parcels. The rail historians accepted the use of some acreage near the North Medford freeway interchange where there were the remains of an obsolete and dismantled but completely cleaned up sewage plant. Thus the name for the railroad. Today the old "digester tank" is filled with granite for use as ballast on the park's tracks. The Live Steamers Club operates the Medford Railroad Park on an agreement with the city.

The main entry-way to the park is open every day, but the railroad part is open for free rides on the 2nd and 4th Sundays between May and September – weather permitting. The area is fenced for protection, has restrooms and good parking. People flock to the Railroad Park on operating days. The club members run up to seven people-carrying trains at a time thus the wait in line for a ride is never long.

Members of the "Steamers" build, own and operate a number of 7½-inch gauge locomotives. These engines weigh between 300 and 3,000 pounds and have values from about $12,000 to about $25,000 each. The locomotives are finished in the colors

Owner-engineer Art Crisp with his model 4-6-2 Pacific.

of major railroads. In the park is a 'car barn" where small passenger cars (adapted to seat riders who straddle each car) are kept. Members are proud of their locomotives, recognize their values, and "we take 'em home at night."

The railroad park is operated by "community cooperation – no charge for rides" but donations, in an old time street car fare box that accepts paper money, are received. Non-cash donations have included tons of granite for ballast. Another firm donated 26,000 precision cut hard wood ties on which the tracks are mounted.

Southern Pacific presented a number of major items for display in the park. These include two semaphore signals, a 1940 caboose and a "flanger." The flanger is a light snow plow that removes snow and ice from the groves in rails and switches. This flanger is one of the permanent exhibits and was used by the S.P. on the Siskiyou Line.

Weyerhaeuser Timber Company donated a caboose previously used on their Oregon, California and Eastern Railway. This line operated between the Weyerhaeuser mill in Klamath

Engineer Gerry Bowden's passengers have just left the cars. He will hold his train until the train ahead is loaded and leaves MacKenzie Station.

Falls over 64 miles of rugged mountains to Bly where there was another Weyerhaeuser mill. This is an ex-S.P. caboose of 1940 vintage.

Medford Corporation provided a hopper car they used in ballasting their tracks. The car, originally a 2-bay ore car has a long local history having been used by the Pacific and Eastern Railroad between Medford and Butte Falls in 1910.

The Rogue Valley Model Railroad Club has put up a building in the park where it is in the process of installing a permanent operating exhibit of tabletop trains. This building is open on the same days the Sewer City Short Line* is hauling its passengers.

With the aid of some important donations, and funds raised by various means, the clubs, working together were able to move the Willamette logging locomotive to the Railroad Park where it is now exhibit. Kids, and adults, still love to climb into the cab and imagine themselves herding the jerky train over the uneven logging railroad track, deep in the forest, pulling a load of freshly cut logs.◇

---

* For the complete story of this passenger-carrying model railroad, refer to the book *The Sewer City Short Line of the Southern Oregon Live Steamers* in bibliography.

Pear Blossom Festival and Races

Representatives of several Medford civic groups, the school district, merchants group, orchardists and the Chamber of Commerce, met in 1954 to initiate an annual spring event that would include the entire city. That first year, a little girl was chosen "Miss Blossom" to lead that first parade of thirty floats and local school bands. Since that time, the Pear Blossom festival, in early April, has grown to involve more than forty organizations with a wide range of activities. These include the Lions Sports Fair, Veterans Hobby Show, Square Dance Jamboree, Orchid Show and the Southern Oregon Philatelic Society's competitive stamp exhibit and bourse. Starting in 1965, the U. S. Postal Service has recognized the Society's popular event and has provided a special postmark and mini-post office during the two day event.

By 1964, motorized floats were admitted to the parade.

Schools from many miles distance plan annual trips to Medford and participation in the parade as the major seasonal trip for their bands and flag drill teams.

Starting in 1977, the Pear Blossom Run has attracted hundreds of distance runners from throughout Oregon as well as from across the nation. ◇

(TOP) **Marching band from Medford's McLoughlin Middle School.** (LOWER) **The speedy adult runners are already out of the gate and down the street in the Pear Blossom Run, followed by hundreds of others of all ages.**

Appendix
The Works of Frank C. Clark

Frank Chamberlain Clark, Architect, designed buildings that were constructed in several Rogue River Valley communities, but they are primarily in Medford. Our list includes all known Clark buildings regardless of where they were built.

Some building have recently been identified as Clark's work through discovery of blueprints, plaques given by the architect at the time, or other characteristics that are identifiable as his work.

Readers are asked to recognize that the accuracy of this list cannot be guaranteed although the intentions of the investigators were honorable. It is plausible that some of the structures may have been demolished or remodeled beyond original recognition. Sources for the investigation included Clark's children, Clark's records, photographs made by Clark, Clark's journals, Clark's notes, newspaper stories, past clients of Clark, Clark's friends. Robert Keeney (partner). Clark designed a number of buildings for clients that were not constructed. Our list may contain some duplications due to conflicting information. An example: the First National Bank/Billings Insurance Company building in Medford shows as No. 31 as well as No. 552.

Our list is in two sections:

1) Frank Clark working alone (1903 - 1937): 258 designs
2) Frank Clark and Robert Keeney (partners after 1938) 45 designs
   Total: 303 designs

The archive for many of Clark's drawings is the Southern Oregon Historical Society in Medford. The Society will appreciate being notified if newly discovered Clark-designed properties are located or if documentable exceptions are noted in our list. *

§ Listed in *National Register of Historic Places*

SITE NUMBER	HISTORIC NAME	ADDRESS	TOWN	GONE
3a	Hotel Medford (original)	406 W. Main	Medford	x
3b	Hotel Medford - 6th Floor addition		Medford	x
3c	Hotel Medford (rebuilt)	406 W. Main	Medford	
5	Medford Elk's Picnic-Casino	Off Agate Road on the Rogue River		x
6	Community Hospital	843 E. Main	Medford	x
7	Gates Auto Company	nw cor 6th &Riverside	Medford	x
9	F. E. Merrick house	839 E. Main	Medford	x
10	James Campbell House	1406 Kings Hwy	Medford	
11	W. B. Biddle House	(location unknown)		
12	Stuart Patterson house	32 Ross Ct	Medford	
14	Perl Funeral Parlor	426 W. 6th St.	Medford	

Two of several Clark-designed buildings at Hillcrest Orchards near the east Medford City Limits

15§(1925)	"Mrs. Bess Young House"	522 S. Oakdale	Medford	
16§(1912)	Charles English house	1006 S. Oakdale	Medford	
17	Root/Banks house	1000 W. Main	Medford	
18	C. I. Hutchinson house	1306 W. Main	Medford	
21§(ca.1919)	Victor Bursell house	3075 Hanley Rd	Central Point	
22§(1919)	Henry van Hoevenberg house	9130 Ramsey Canyon Rd	Sams Valley	
23§(ca.1905)	Evans/Mattern house	206 Hargadine Rd	Ashland	
24§(1910)	Humbolt Pracht house	234 Vista	Ashland	
25	Medford City Fire Hall	nw cor N. Front & W 3rd	Medford	x
26	Paulina B. Clark house	25 Summit	Medford	
27	Frank C & Grace W. Clark house	1007 W 10th	Medford	
29	H. D. Norton house	408 S. Oakdale	Medford	
31	First National Bank/ Billings Insurance Co.	E. Main & Oak	Medford	
32a	Medford Senior High Sch (Renamed South Medford High School)	815 S. Oakdale	Medford	
32b	Stadium Bleachers - High Sch	815 S. Oakdale	Medford	
33§(ca.1931)	Clark/Jackson house	1917 E. Main	Medford	
35§(ca.1912)	Ralph Bardwekk house	1002 S. Oakdale	Medford	
36§(1937)	J. P. Naumes house	1001 S. Oakdale	Medford	
37§(1916)	Delroy Getchell house	1121 .S. Oakdale	Medford	
39	Donald McKee house	8 Geneva St	Medford	
40	George Porter house	826 Minnesota	Medford	
41§(1922)	H. A. Thierolf house	828 Minnesota	Medford	
42	Louis Ulrich house	839 Minnesota	Medford	
43§(1909)	E. V. Carter house	514 Siskiyou	Ashland	
44	Geo. Tavenber house	912 Siskiyou	Ashland	
45	Walter Bowne house	1845-? Old State Rd	Central Point	
46a	Hillcrest Orchard – Parson House	3285 Hillcrest	Medford rural	
46b	Hillcrest Orchard – Office Bldg		Medford rural	
46c	Hillcrest Orchard – New barn		Medford rural	
46d	Hillcrest Orchard – Supt's house		Medford rural	
46e	Hillcrest Orchard – Tank & Pump house		Medford rural	
47	Leverett Bldg.	1115-121 S. Central	Medford	
48a	H. D. McCasky house	2910 Table Rock Rd	Medford	
48b	H. D. McCasky barn		Medford	
48c	H. D. McCasky garage		Medford	
50	Medford Elks Temple	202 N. Central	Medford	
51	I.O.O.F. Bldg	221 W 6th	Medford	x
53	Littrel Bldg	319 E 6th	Medford	
56a	Medford Airport –Adm Bldg	Biddle Rd	Medford rural	

56b	Medford Airport – hangar		Medford rural	
58	Holly Theater	222 W 6th	Medford	
59	Sparta Bldg	405 E. Main	Medford	
62§(1909)	F. K. Duel house	1018 S. Oakdale	Medford	
63	Cooley Bldg (Craterian Theater)	39 S. Central	Medford	
64	Fluhrer Bldg (remodel)	se cor E. Main & S.Central	Medford	x
67	Fluhrer Bakery Bldg	29 N. Holly	Medford	·
69	Garnet-Corey Bldg	502 W. Main	Medford	
70b	Cargill Court Apts	331 W 6th	Medford	x
75	Medford Airport Bldg	S. Pacific Hwy	Medford rural	x
78	Bear Creek Orchard Adm Bldg	2518 S. Pacific Hwy	Medford rural	
79§(1904)	Chappel-Swedenburg house	990 Siskiyou	Ashland	
80a	Barnum Hotel	204 N Front	Medford	
80b	Barnum Hotel garage	(unknown location)		x
80c	Barnum Hotel Sample Room	(unknown location)		x
82	A. C. Hough house	707 NW "A"	Grants Pass	
83	Greater Medford Community House (unknown location)			
86§(1928)	O. O. Alendorfer house	718 S. Oakdale	Medford	
87§(1912)	Geo. Triechler house	995 S. Oakdale	Medford	
90	Medford Natatorium	E side of N. Riverside nr Jackson	Medford	x
92	Chauncy M. Brewer house	1811 E. Main	Medford	
93	T. E. Daniels house	1805 E. Main	Medford	
94	Roland Hubbard house	831 Minnesota	Medford	
97	Civic Club House	59 Winburn Way	Ashland	
98	Ashland Elks Bldgs	255 E. Main	Ashland	
99	Enders Bldg	250 E. Main	Ashland	
100§	Michael Clemens house	612 NW 3rd	Grants Pass	
101§(1909)	George Clemens house	612 NW 5th	Grants Pass	
103	Geo. Roberts house	1815 Crown	Medford	
105	L. A. Salade house	(unknown address)	Central Point	
107	"Timber room"	se cor E. main & S. Riverside	Medford	
111	Ernest Barnes house	1906 E. Main	Medford	
114	Cornelius Collins house	1810 E. Main	Medford	
117	Rialto Theater Bldg	123 W. Main	Medford	x
118	Swedenburg Bldg.	200 Block - E. Main	Ashland	
119	Charles Rose house	550 E. Main	Ashland	
120a	So. Ore. Normal Sch	Siskiyou	Ashland	x
120b	So. Ore. Normal Sch - gymnasium		Ashland	x
123	Robert Conroy house	200 Medford Hgts	Medford	
124	Clancy house	204 Medford Hgts	Medford	
125	Washington Grade Sch	610 S. Peach	Medford	
131	John A. Fluhrer house	2447 Hillcrest	Medford	
132	W. Henry Fluhrer house	112 Scheffel	Medford	
133	Bruce Bauer house	1336 Queen Anne	Medford	
134	Vaupel, Beebe & Kinney Bldg	31-33 N. Main	Ashland	
135a	Masonic Bldg (remodel)	27 N. Main	Ashland	
135b	Masonic Bldg (remodel)	27 N. Main	Ashland	
136	Gerald A. Cottingham house	1329 Queen Anne	Medford	
139§ (1905)	Wm. M. Poley house	64 Gresham	Ashland	
142	W. H. Lydiard house	16 Geneva	Medford	
143	Humphrey & Sons Bldg	534 E. Main	Medford	

146	Ashland Creamery Bldg.	Winburn at Lithia Park	Ashland	x
147	Gwin Butler house	41 Granite	Ashland	
151	Granite City Com. Hospital	Palm & Siskiyou	Ashland	x
153	Community Bldg	340 S. Pioneer	Ashland	
157	(Three story business block)	(unknown address)	Ashland	x
159	Hargrove Business Block	Main & First	Ashland	x
162	Temple of Truth Church	479 Siskiyou	Ashland	x
163	Ashland Improvement Co. Bldg.	25 N Main	Ashland	
164	Ashland Natatorium	Fist & Spring	Ashland	x
165	Albert Bldg.	108½ N 6th	Grants Pass	
166	Paddock Bldg.	207 S.6th	Grants Pass	
167	Calvert Bldg.	___ S. 6th	Grants Pass	
168	Hunt & Antle Theater	6th & "S"	Grants Pass	x
169	E. H. Janney house	6 N. Modoc	Medford	
171	Mason Ehrman Warehouse	340 N. Fir	Medford	x
172	Frank Owens house	1507 E. Main	Medford	
173	"Bohemian Club"	105-111 N. Fir and W. Main	Medford	
174	Crater Lake Garage	103 S. Riverside	Medford	
176	Charles Conner house	(unknown location)		
177	C. E. Gates house	1307 Queen Anne	Medford	
178	Pinnacle Packing House	441 S. Fir	Medford	x
179	American Fruit Growers Bldg	East side S. Fir btwn 9th and 10th	Medford	x
180	Charles. Newhall house (alt.)	2748 Old stage Rd	Central Point	
181	Constance Ames house(alt)	423 Park	Ashland	
183	Henry Judge house (alt)	410 E. "D"	Jacksonville	
189a	Page Theater (interior - alt)	E. Main nr Bear Creek	Medford	x
189b	Page Theater	-do-	Medford	x
189c	Page Theater	-do-	Medford	x
190	Albert Orr house	220 Barneburg	Medford	
191	E. R. Lamport house	S. Pacific Hwy	Medford rural	
197	Marjorie Feasley house	1820 Crown	Medford	
221	Elk Trail School	Elk Creek Rd	Trail	
227	Wagner Creek School	8448 Wagner Creek Rd	Talent	
229	Otis Booth House	Suncrest Rd	Talent	
235	Everett G. Trowbridge house	3237 Jacksonville Hwy	Medford rural	
249	Albert Stratton house	2865 Hanley Rd	Central Point	
254	Madden/McCasky house	3347 Old State Rd	Central Point	
259	Ashland Exhibit Booth	nr Railroad Depot	Ashland	x
264	Jackson County Fair Bldgs	South Pacific Hwy	Medford	x
265	Thomas Petch house	3654 S. Pacific Hwy	Phoenix	
266	Ed. Miller house	(adse unknown) S. Pacific Hwy	Phoenix	
272a	Roosevelt School addition	112 Lindley	Medford	
274	A. L. Aiken Bldg.	281 E. Main	Medford	
294	Merkle house	39 Summit	Medford	
295	_____	1222 W. Main	Medford	
297	Geo. Murphy Ranch (house alteration)	nr McCloud Br on Rogue River		
298	F. L. Foster Bldg.	200 block - E. Main	Ashland	
301	F. L. Camps Bldg	54 E. Main	Ashland	
303	Dodge Furn & Carpets Bldg	123 E. Main	Ashland	
304	Frank Strickfaden House	145 Almond	Ashland	
305	John Chambers house	137 Almond	Ashland	

306	C. W. Holmes Bldg.	97 N. Main	Ashland	
309	John Jensen house	508 Park	Medford	
311	Firestone Bldg.	33 S. Riverside	Medford	
312	C. C. Wing Bldg.	4th & "B"	Ashland	x
315	(Business block)	"North of Plaza" Main St	Ashland	x
317	Masonic Bldg. remodel	218½ W. Main	Medford	x
318	City Hall/Interim Courthouse	Front & 5th	Medford	x
319	YWCA addition	200 Block - Bartlett	Medford	x
320	Eagle Point High School	---	Eagle Point	
321a	Medford High Sch Main Bldg	3209 W. 2nd	Medford	
	(Renamed McLoughlin Jr. High Sch)			
321b	Medford High School Manual Arts Bldg		Medford	
	(Renamed McLoughlin Jr. High Sch)			
321c	Medford High School Gymnasium		Medford	
	(Renamed McLoughlin Jr. High Sch)			
322	J. J. Emmens house remodel	1443 E. Main	Medford	
323	Frederick Johnson house remodel	2322 E. Main	Medford	
324	A. L. Livingston house remodel	4132 Livingston Rd	Jacksonville	
326	Raymond Driver house	4140 Old State Rd	Central Point	
327	Pacific Home Telephone Bldg	131 Bartlett	Medford	
328	Christian Science Church	23 S. Pioneer	Ashland	
329	*Main Tribune* Bldg.	21 N. Fir	Medford	x
331	Gilbert Stuart house	18 Modic	Medford	
333	Central Point Presbyterian Church	100 Oak	Central Point	
	(Now First Baptist Ch of Central Point)			
335	Trail School	--	Trail	
337	W. m. Shephard house	2003 Hillcrest	Medford	
340	COPCO Bldg. addition	216 Main	Ashland	
343	Osteopathic Clinic Bldg	200 Block E. Jackson	Medford	
346	Bert Elliot house	5 Corning Ct.	Medford	
353	Houston Brother's house	(unknown location)		
354	Fred T. Lewis house	(unknown location)		
355	Mrs. A. Holloway house	(unknown location)		
361	Episcopal Church	5th & Oakdale	Medford	
363	Rosenbaum/Reames Bldg	436 W. Main	Medford	
388	John C. Mann house	815 E. Main	Medford	
389	Max GeBauer house	15 Corning Ct	Medford	
390	Fred Heath Sr. House	820 E. Main	Medford	
395	Josephine County Fair Bldgs	--	Grants Pass	x
396	Lutheran Church	508 4th	Medford	
397	Howard School	2801 Merriman Rd	Medford	
398	June Earhart house	945 S. Riverside	Medford	
399	Victor Mills house	155 Strawberry Ln	Ashland	
400	B. E. Harder house	3531 Ross Ln	Central Point	
404	F. W. Townsend house	3188 Ross Ln	Central Point	
407	Fred Scheffel house	2501 Lyman	Medford	
411	Hotel Josephine remodel	6th & "E"	Grants Pass	x
413	Bert Anderson house	1501 W. Main	Medford	
428	Rogue River Lodge	--	Shady Cove	
435§(1926)	Larry Shade house	979 S. Oakdale	Medford	
445	"The Frame House"	1960 W. Main	Medford	
446	___	Bellinger Ln nr Hull Rd	Medford rural	

452	G. F. Billings Insurance Agency Bldg	45 E. Main	Ashland	
459	---	Peach	Medford	x
484	Dr. Sewn house	(unknown location)		
485	Enders house	(unknown location)		
486	Wm. S. Barnum	1684 Spring	Medford	
487	T. Simpson	(unknown location)		
489	McDonough	(unknown location)		
491	Wm. Young	815 Bennett	Medford	x
493	Jackson County Warehouse	(unknown location)		
494	V. Katrina	(unknown location)		
495	Snider	(unknown location)		
496	Floyd Hart/Milton Snow house	3817 Grant Rd	Central Point	
497	William Bates	unsure) 32 Geneva	Medford	
498	Mrs. Julia Doubleday	(unsure) 202 Portland	Medford	
499	American Laundry Bldg	(unsure) 132 S. Central	Medford	
500	Scott V. Davis	(unsure) Main & Central	Medford	
501	Hannon (or Hansen) Bldg	(unknown location)		
503	Mrs. Gerdes	(unsure) 123 Vancouver	Medford	
504	Southern Oregon Gas Co. Bldg	(unknown location)		
505	P. L Andrews	(unknown location)		
506	Jacksonville School alteration	--	Jacksonville	
507	Talent School Gymnasium	--	Talent	
508	Woodsmen Building	143 N. Grape	Medford	
510	Wm. Yerky Apartment	N. Pacific Hwy	Medford rural	
511	Carl Rau Auto Court		Central Point	x
	(Believed to have been where 7-Eleven store is — S. Front & N. Pacific Hwy.)			
512	Oldsmobile Sales & Service Bldg		Central Point	x
	(Believed to have been in 300 block E. Pine, presently occupied by 1st Inter-State Bank)			
513	Glen Simpson house	(on w. side Ashland St)	Medford	
515	Harvey J. Field Bldg	344 N. Bartlett	Medford	
516	Central Point First National Bank	(unknown location)	Central Point	
518	United Airlines Passenger Depot	Airport – Biddle Rd	Medford	
520	Pacific Co-op Poultry Producers of Portland	(address unknown)	Grants Pass	
524	Charles A. Wing Bldg	se cor 4th & Central	Medford	
526	Putnam/Athey house	(address unknown)	Central Point	
528	W. E. Hammell house	Crater Lake hwy	Medford rural	
529	Glen Clymer house	(unknown location)		
532	Jorgen Jorgenson house	1913 Hillcrest	Medford	
533	John Moffatt house	34 N. Berkeley Way	Medford	
534	L. P. Older house	38 N. Berkeley Way	Medford	
535	Mrs. B. E. Canode house	1716 Crown	Medford	
536	Mel Hogan house	1512 E. Main	Medford	
537	James Pulver Motel	1237 N. Riverside	Medford	
538	Neff house	ne cor Barneburg & Hillcrest	Medford	
___	Ben Trowbridge Sr.	202 N. Bartlett	Medford	
539	Porter Lumber Co residence	ne cor Queen Anne & Lindley	Medford	
540	Roland Birkholz house	Myers Ln	Medford rural	
541	___	1325 Bundy	Medford	
542§(ca.1930)	Quisenberry house	715 S. Oakdale	Medford	
544	"Blackwell Hill" School	(no information)		
545	Shady Cove School	--	Shady Cove	

(ABOVE AND ON PAGE 170) **Many Clark-designed residences are now sheltered so well by trees, the buildings are often difficult to view.**

546	Pinehurst School	15337 Hwy 66	Pinehurst	
547	Groceteria	100 block N. Central	Medford	x
548	Groceteria (early super-market)	100 block N. Grape	Medford	
	(Now: Jackson County Educational Service Dist. Headquarters)			
549	Greyhound Bus Depot	212 N. Bartlett	Medford	
550	Porter Neff Bldg.	ne cor 6th & N. Central	Medford	
551	First National Bank/Billings Insurance Co.	--	Medford	
552	First State Bank of Eagle Point remodel	(address unknown)	Eagle Point	
	(*See also*: No. 31)			
553	(Business Block)	ne cor 6th & Bartlett	Medford	
__	A. Evan Reames house	10th & Newton	Medford	

Buildings Designed After 1938

30	L.B./ W. J. W arner house remodel	519 S. Oakdale	Medford	
65	Goldy Bldg remodel	107 W. Main	Medford	
66	Kay Bldg	34 S. Dir	Medford	
68	YMCA - addition	522 W. Main	Medford	
73	Medford Bowling Lanes	821 N. Riverside	Medford	
74	Big Y Shopping Center	nw cor Table Rock Rd & N. Hwy 99	Medford	x
	(This supermarket was totally demolished - now location of Ray's Foodplace supermarket)			
77	Shetler/Henselman house	35 S. Berkeley Way	Medford	
81	Lithia Theater	166 E. Main	Ashland	
96	Eugene Bennett Apartment	337 S. Grape	Medford	
106	Porter/Norris house	1900 Hillcrest	Medford	
109	Gilhousen house	2001 E. Main	Medford	
110	W. G. Garner house	2009 E. Main	Medford	
112	Roy Harper house	7 Glen Oak	Medford	
115	Walter Hoppe house	1806 E. Main	Medford	

144	Mrs. E. P. Power house	100 vancouver	Medford
182	Roberts house	ne cor Black Oak & Acorn	Medford
185	Eugene D. Thorndyke house	55 S. Berkeley	Medford
186	Parsons Hunting Lodge		Howard Prairie Lake
188	Johnson/Trowbridge house	1625 E. Main	Medford
192	Berwick Wood house	2445 E. Main	Medford
193	W. B. Sherman house remodel	(unknown location)	Grants Pass
194	Gain Robinson house	(unknown location)	Medford
195	Kingdom Hall	(unknown location)	Medford
196	F. W. Tevins house	113 Valley View	Medford
198	Edward Kubli house	1138 Applegate Road	rural
199	Porter Lumber Co. Bldg.	sw cor Fir & 9th	Medford
200	C. L. Moore house	(unknown location)	Ashland
201	Cleo Haley Young house	3249 Willow Springs Rd	Central Point
202	Otto Frohnmayer house	1656 Spring	Medford
203	Medford School Admin Bldg	500 Monroe	Medford
204	T. F. Pulver house	(address unknown)	Medford
205	Nye & Naumes Bldg	(address unknown)	Medford
206	Riverside Motel	971 SE 6th	Grants Pass
207	Josephine Bank	--	Grants Pass
208	Chris Schempf Bldg	(address unknown)	Central Point
210	V. F. W. Bldg (adse unknown - vicinity E. 8th at Bear Cr. west of creek)		Medford
211	T. L. Shoop house	(address unknown)	Medford
212	Lincoln School Addition (Now: Cornerstone Church and School)	608 N. Bartlett	Medford
314	Harry Holmes house	___ Modoc	Medford
332	Thompson house	(no data)	
___	Medford Ice & Cold Storage	315 S. Fir	Medford1 x
352	Reed Tractor & Equip Bldg	(unknown location)	
429	Jean Cameron house	2946 Cedar Links	Medford
521	George Harrington house	208 Bradford	Medford
___	Stuart McQueen house	2136 Hillcrest	Medford

Short Takes Around Town

Medford has no many exciting things to see and do that to attempt to list all would turn this book into a combination Yellow Pages of the telephone book and a Chamber of Commerce spiel combined. Here are a token few, in any order.

Rogue Valley Mall

The Rogue Valley Mall, near the North Medford freeway inter-change, sees early morning walkers the year around but especially in winter when frigid weather and rains come. The mall is home to dozens of businesses large and small.

The Medford *Mail Tribune*

Press Room

Medford's newspaper, the *Mail Tribune*, celebrated its 90th birthday in 1996 with a street party of jazz bands, refreshments, and tours of its new offices and plant. It is an independent daily newspaper and is a division of Ottoway Newspapers, Inc. This Pulitzer Prize winning paper uses the wire service of the Associated Press. The paper has a week day average circulation of 28,000. It's Friday edition numbers 36,000 and Sunday 34,000.

This church model reed organ, a Peloubet, was purchased from Lyon & Healy Company in Chicago in 1893 by the Methodist Church in Ashland. In 1929 it was sold to the Presbyterians in Phoenix, Oregon. The compressed air that operates this organ was supplied by a hand-operated pump but the Presbyterians added an electric motor to do this. Eventually, the organ was acquired by the Southern Oregon Historical Society. Its appearance is deceptive as the pipes across the front are only decorative. These display pipes cause casual observers to believe this is a pipe organ which it is not. The organ is playable. Concerts, in the historical society's museum in Medford, are often presented during the winter holiday season.

FIRST PRESBYTERIAN CHURCH

There are churches in Medford representing the major denominations and there are many independents. All of them welcome new people. The Presbyterian Church, a major centrally located church, has a specific downtown mission statement:

We are a committed, caring congregation that is determined to be a vital presence in the downtown community and the world through creative worship and the development of a relevant understanding of our faith as followers of Christ.

More and more golf links are being built, some 9-hole, others 18-hole.

Planting House Seed

Medford's residential neighborhoods are growing as fast as builders can develop them.

Bibliography

Books

Atwood, Kay. *An Honorable History; 133 years of Medical Practice in Jackson County, Oregon.* Private print. 1985.

Beeson, Welborn. *The Diary of Welborn Beeson on the Oregon & Applegate Trails in 1853.* Webb Research Group. 1993.

Best, Gerald M and David L. Joslyn. "Locomotives of the Southern Pacific Company" in *Bulletin No. 94.* Railway and Locomotive Historical Society. Boston. 1956.

Burkhardt, D. C. Jesse. *Backwoods Railroads; Branchlines and Shortlines of Western Oregon.* Wash .State Univ. Press. 1994.

Ledward, Kay. *The History of Library Services in Medford and Jackson County.* Unpub ms. [1965].

Lindbergh, Charles A. *The Spirit of St. Louis.* Scribner's. 1953.

_____. *The War-time Journals of Charles A. Lindbergh.* Harcourt. 1970.

Milligan, George E. *We Fly the White Birds; Observations of Mercy Flights [Air Ambulance].* Webb Research Group. 1983.

Rhinehart, Rosalyn R. *The Beginnings of the Rogue Valley.* Privately published. 1990.

Snedicor, Jane. *History of Medford.* Unpub. ms. 1935.

Webber, Bert. *People and Notes, The Southern Oregon Symphonic Band and its Predecessor The Hillah Temple Shrine Band.* Reflected Images Publishers. 1994.

_____. *Over the Applegate Trail to Oregon in 1846.* Webb Research Group. 1996.

Webber, Bert and Margie. *Jacksonville Oregon, Antique Town in a Modern Age.* Webb Research Group. 1994.

_____. *Oregon's Great Train Holdup, Bandits Murder 4 — Didn't Get A Dime; Documentary.* Webb Research Group. 1988.

_____. *Railroading in Southern Oregon and the Founding of Medford.* YeGalleon. 1985.

_____. *The Sewer City Short Line of the Southern Oregon Live Steamers.* Webb Research Group. 1993.

_____. *This Is Logging and Sawmilling – Documentary.* Webb Research Group. 1996.

_____. *Single-Track to Jacksonville; The Rogue River Valley Railway and the Southern Oregon Traction Company - Documentary.* Webb Research Group. 1990.

Newspapers, magazines and special reports

Abbot, Henry L. "Report of Lieut. Henry L. Abbot, Corps of Top. Engrs, Upon Exploration For A Railroad…[in] 1865." in *Senate Executive Document No., 78*, 33rd Congress. 2d Session, 1857. U.S. Gov Print Office. 1857.

Becker, Hattie B. *The History of Rogue Valley International–Medford* [airport]. Private print (Jackson County Airport Authority). 1995.

"City Established as Medical Center" in *Mail Tribune.* June 5, 1985.

Hamilton, Eva. "Editor Robert W. Ruhl and the Pulitzer Award," in *Mail Tribune.* Apr. 28, 1975.

The History and Status of Artificial Fog Dispersal [at Medford…]. United Air Lines Special Studies No. 110. Private print. Jan. 6, 1964.

Hutchinson, Peggy Ann. "Fog Dispersal Practiced at Medford-Jackson Port," in *Humboldt Beacon.* Dec. 9. 1976.

_____. "Early Ordinances of Medford Relate Story of Growing City," in *Mail Tribune.* April 7, 1963.

"Lindbergh Here for Brief Visit Enroute North" in *Mail Tribune.* Jul. 5, 1939.

Reiss, Al. "She's Still Dancing in Our hearts; Graceful Ginger [Rogers] Takes Final Call From the World's Greatest Caster" in *Mail Tribune.* Apr. 26, 1995.

"Techniques of Fog Dispersal Explained at Meeting Here" in *Mail Tribune.* July 5, 1964.

Watson, Stu. "Mabel Ruhl Puts High Value on MT Public Role," in *Mail Tribune.* Oct. 29, 1981.

Webber, Bert. "Here's Smudge in Your Eye" (Series - two parts) Part I. Orchardists Have Real 'Spring Fever'" in *Oregon Journal* May 19, 1970; Part II. "Almost Everybody Recognizes This Pollution Problem" in *Oregon Journal.* May 20, 1970.

_____. "Never Say Die "(Series - two parts) Part I. "State of Jefferson Secession Gets New Shot In T-Shirt" in *Oregon Journal.* Dec. 6, 1971; Part II. "State of Jefferson 'Up-Staged' By Pearl Harbor Attack" in *Oregon Journal.* Dec. 7, 1971.

"Wings Over Oregon; A Salute to Half Century of Aviation" in *Mail Tribune.* Sec. C. Sept. 14, 1976.

About the Authors

Bert Webber traces his earliest interest in writing to a day when he was caught laying out a miniature newspaper front page on the back of an arithmetic paper in the 5th grade.

As a research photojournalist and a book designer, he writes and publishes books about what he calls the "fantastic Pacific Northwest."

After studying at the University of Nevada, be graduated in Journalism from Whitworth College in Spokane then earned the Master of Library Science degree after studies at Portland State University and the University of Portland. For several years he taught journalism and history and was a school librarian in Washington and Oregon. During World War-II, splitting his duty between the Signal Corps and Air Force, he served in Alaska, England, Scotland, Belgium and in France.

Bert has photographed more subjects than he can remember, has written hundreds of articles for newspapers and periodicals and he has written about sixty books.

Margie Webber is a retired Registered Nurse who earned her baccalaureate degree in Nursing from the University of Washington. She has worked in a wide variety of professional nursing positions and was a consultant in nutrition and skin care. She has contributed to professional papers. On books, she assists in field research, photography, and serves as a copy editor and proof reader. She is co-author of a number of books.

The Webbers make their home in the town of Central Point a few miles north of Medford and which, like Medford, is built on the Agate Desert. They have four children and eight grandchildren. ◇

Index

Page numbers for pictures and maps are shown in *bold italic* type